A TRUE STORY

RISE AGAIN

My journey from high school dropout
to obtaining a doctorate

DR ALI SHERAZI

About the Author

Dr Ali Sherazi is a bestselling author, inspirational speaker, entrepreneur and widely followed social media personality known for his message of hope, resilience and transformation.

From being a high school dropout to obtaining a doctorate, Dr Sherazi's trajectory reflects perseverance against the odds. Beginning as a cleaner in the local juice shop in Rawalpindi, Pakistan, he is now a global speaker, a CEO and the force behind the Ali Sherazi Foundation. His foundation supports vulnerable communities, promotes education and is building a Baitul Noor House for orphans.

Through his extraordinary personal story and uplifting work, Dr Sherazi has grown his international audience to over 6.5 million followers. This has made him one of the most influential motivational voices for audiences seeking inspiration, personal growth and renewed purpose.

Dr Sherazi's first book, *Suno Tum Sitare Ho (Listen! You Are a Star)*, was published in Urdu and distributed internationally, becoming a record-selling success throughout Pakistan, where he currently resides. His second book, *Rise Again*, will be published in English by Hembury Books.

A catalogue record for this book is available from the National Library of Australia

Dedicated!
to my parents

To those who guided me at every step of life,
taught me to live with discipline, and blessed me
with selfless love and self-confidence,
I am deeply grateful to my parents.

They gave me the lesson of humanity that
introduced me to the true purpose of my life.

I humbly pray to the One and Only God
to grant my parents a long life filled with
health and well-being. Ameen.

Endorsements for *Rise Again*

"*Rise Again* is an inspiring story of resilience, hope, and transformation. Dr Ali Sherazi's journey is a strong reminder that setbacks do not define a person's future. What matters is the courage to keep going, learn, and turn adversity into growth. This book offers an encouraging message for anyone who has ever felt behind, discouraged, or doubtful of their potential."

Nick Bracks
Author, Speaker, Founder of Move Your Mind
Melbourne, Australia

"*Rise Again* is a moving and uplifting account of perseverance, self-belief, and personal transformation. Dr Ali Sherazi shares a journey that will resonate with readers who have faced disappointment, hardship, or uncertainty in life. His story shows that with determination, faith, and continued effort, it is possible to rise above circumstances and create a meaningful future. This book is both heartfelt and encouraging."

Emma Richardson
Author and Acadamic
United Kingdom

Contents

Rise Again

Some books are written to impress.

This book is written to pull you back up.

If you are reading this, there is a chance you have felt the weight of failure—failure in study, failure in career, failure in confidence, failure in relationships, failure in discipline, or simply failure in believing in yourself. Maybe you started late. Maybe you fell behind. Maybe people around you made you feel like you will never catch up.

I know that feeling—because I lived it.

Failing in high school was a tough experience for me. It felt like everyone was judging me, and I got labeled as a failure. People would say things like, "You're just not cut out for this," or "You're not smart enough." Those words really hurt, and sometimes they can be overwhelming. You start to believe that you're not good enough, and that failure is who you are. It's like, you begin to think that you're defined by this one thing that didn't go right. But the truth is, failure is not the end of the world. It's not who you are as a person. It's just something that happened, and it doesn't have to define your future.

But I learned something that changed my life:

Failure is an event. It is not a destiny.

Getting back on track wasn't easy for me. It didn't start with a big celebration or anything like that. It started with a tough decision - a quiet one, but a hard one to make: I'm going to try again. I went back to studying, even when it felt weird. I built up my confidence, one small step at a time. There were times when I just didn't feel like it, but I kept going anyway. And after a while, with a lot of hard work and discipline, I finally reached my goal - something that people had told me was impossible: getting my doctorate. It wasn't always easy, but it was worth it. I had to push myself, even when I didn't feel like it. But in the end, it all paid off.

But my journey wasn't only about education.

I still recall the early days of my social media journey; it was a real test of my patience. At one point, I only had 38 followers, which was pretty discouraging. I even asked a classmate to follow me, just so I could get to 39. I was putting my heart and soul into creating content, posting videos and writing posts, but it seemed like no one was paying attention. I'd get zero views or just a few, and that silence was deafening. It's tough not to take it personally and start questioning your self-worth and the direction you're heading in. But I didn't let it break me.

Yet I kept going.

I've come a long way in terms of getting my message across, delivering it in a way that resonates, and being consistent. One of the biggest things I've learned is to stay strong and patient, even when I wasn't seeing the results I wanted right away. But the thing is, consistency really does pay off - over time, it's led to some amazing growth. I feel really lucky to have had the support of so many people, and I'm grateful for the opportunity to have reached such a huge audience. Today, my videos have been viewed hundreds of millions of times - we're talking over 500 million views across all my content - and my following has grown from just a small group of people to millions. It's been an incredible journey, and I'm thankful for everything I've learned along the way.

Then came another test: writing a book.

When my first book, *Listen, You Are a Star*, came out, it wasn't exactly met with open arms by everyone. In fact, it was rejected and doubted by some people. But I learned a valuable lesson from that experience: rejection isn't the end of the road — it's often just the beginning of something even better. And that's exactly what happened with my book. It went on to become a record-seller in Pakistan, which just goes to show that sometimes when the world says "no", it's only because it's getting ready to say a bigger "yes" later on. You see, rejection can be tough to deal with, but it can also be a turning point that sets you on a path to something amazing. So, even though my book wasn't welcomed with open arms at first, it ultimately found its way to success, and that's a lesson I'll always carry with me.

So why did I write *Rise Again*?

Because I have met too many people who are talented, but broken by failure. Too many people who have potential, but lost in doubt. Too many people who are alive, but not truly living, because fear and shame have made them small.

This book is for anyone who feels behind in life.

For anyone who has failed and wants to rise again.

For anyone who is tired of motivation that feels good for one day and disappears the next.

Here's what it really means to be successful: it's not just about having a lot of money or being famous. It's about becoming a better version of yourself, someone who is strong, disciplined, and knows what they want. You'll learn that a dream is just a dream until you start taking action and working towards it every day. This book is based on a true story, and it will show you how to turn your struggles into something that drives you forward. You'll find out how to stay positive even when things seem impossible, how to make a plan and stick to it, and how to keep going even when you don't see results right away. The most important thing you'll learn is how to pick yourself up after you've failed and keep moving forward. You'll discover how to stop making excuses and start taking responsibility for your life, how to focus on finding solutions instead of getting bogged down in problems, and how to learn from the times when you're rejected or things don't go your way. By reading this book, you'll get the tools you need to build discipline and start achieving your goals, one step at a time. You'll be able to apply the same principles that helped me turn my life around, and you'll be able to rise above your challenges and create the life you want.

As you go through these lessons, you'll also get to read about my own personal story - from dropping out to earning a doctorate, from being silent to becoming visible, and from facing rejection to achieving record sales. This will show you, time and time again, one important message that stands out.

It is possible to begin again. And begin again. And win.

A promise to the reader
I am not writing this to tell you that life is easy. It isn't.
I am writing to tell you something more powerful:
You are not finished.
If you have failed, you are not a loser—you are a person with a lesson.
If you are behind, you are not weak—you are simply not done.
If you feel stuck, it does not mean your life is stuck.

This book will challenge you, push you, and rebuild your confidence, not with fantasy, but with practical principles and real experience.

So, take a deep breath.

You are not here by accident.

This is your reminder, and this is your moment:

Rise Again.

The Journey: The Path to Success

Success isn't something you reach one day and then feel like you've made it. It's more like a journey, with ups and downs, twists and turns. Sometimes you know where you're going, but often you're not really sure. And no matter what, it's always asking something of you - to learn, to adapt, and to grow. A lot of people don't achieve their goals because they're missing something, but it's not usually talent. It's because they think of success as a dream, rather than a path they need to follow every day. They want the end result, without putting in the effort, the recognition without doing the hard work, and the praise without making sacrifices. But the truth is, the journey itself is what makes success worth having. When you accept that, things get real, and you start to grow as a person. You become stronger, more resilient, and more honest with yourself. The path to success isn't easy, but it's the only way to get there. And when you're on that path, you'll find that it's not just about achieving your goals, but about who you become along the way.

I know how hard it can be to start something new. My own journey was tough at first. I didn't feel confident, I felt unsure and overwhelmed. There were a lot of people who didn't think I could do it, and to be honest, sometimes I didn't think I could do it either. But I took small steps, even when they seemed too small to make a difference. And you know what? Those small steps ended up being the foundation of everything I've achieved. The thing is, the start of any journey is rarely exciting. It's usually hard and it feels like you're starting from scratch. You might feel like giving up when people don't believe in you, or when you're not seeing the results, you want right away. And sometimes, your own mind can be your worst enemy, making you doubt yourself and your abilities. But here's the thing: you don't have to feel ready to start. You just have to be willing to move forward, even when you're scared, even when you're not perfect, and even when you're still learning. It's okay to be afraid and unsure, because that's all part of the journey. And the truth is, the journey to success is not about being perfect, it's about being brave enough to take that first step, and then the next, and the next. So, don't wait until you feel ready, because the truth is, you'll never feel fully ready. Just start, and trust that the rest will follow.

So, you want to know the secret to getting somewhere in life? It all starts with having a clear direction. Lots of people aren't really failing, they're just not sure what they want. One day they're all about learning, the next they're trying to start a business, and the day after that they're chasing fame. Then, they just give up on everything. To make progress, you need to know where you're headed, at least for the next few steps. Having a direction helps you focus, and when you're focused, you can turn your efforts into real progress. When you choose a path, you stop wandering aimlessly and wasting your energy on things that don't matter. You stop letting your emotions and distractions control you. You start walking with purpose, like someone who knows exactly where they're going, even if the journey is long.

The second key is routine. Success is not built by rare motivation; it is built by common routines. Motivation comes and goes, but routine stays. Your routine must become stronger than your mood. On good days, routine protects consistency. On bad days, routine protects your future. When you build a simple daily routine around learning, discipline, and improvement, you start creating a new identity. And identity is powerful, because when you see yourself as a person who shows up daily, your results eventually have no choice but to change.

The third key is learning how to measure progress correctly. Many people quit because they measure progress in the wrong units. They chase views before skill, money before value, and recognition before consistency. In the early stage, your job is not to chase big results. Your job is to build capacity. You must ask yourself: Am I improving? Am I learning faster? Am I becoming more disciplined? Am I becoming better than I was last month? When you keep improving, results become a matter of time. The world eventually notices the person who refuses to stop growing.

Succeeding in life is a real journey, and it needs a new way of looking at failure. Failure can be painful, but it's not the end - it's more like a guide. It shows you what you need to change, where your plan is not working, and where you need to be stronger. When things don't go as planned, don't think "I've had enough." Instead, think "I'm learning something new." This small change in how you think can turn failures into lessons and obstacles into opportunities. It's not about avoiding the tough times, but about learning from them, that's how strong people are made. They don't give up when things get hard, they keep going and use those experiences to get stronger.

As you journey through life, it's crucial to safeguard your thoughts and ideas. Not everyone has your best interests at heart, and some people may try to bring you down because they can't envision a brighter future for you. Others might be uncomfortable with your progress, while some may fear the changes that come with your growth. If you listen to every negative voice, you'll lose touch with your own inner guidance. That's why the company you keep and the things you expose yourself to are so important. What you watch, what you listen to, who you surround yourself with, and what you repeat to yourself all have a profound impact on your mindset. And your mindset, in turn, shapes your actions and decisions. So, protect your mind with the same care and attention that you would your finances, because your mind is your most valuable asset. Remember, your thoughts and beliefs have the power to either limit or liberate you, so choose wisely what you allow into your mental space. By being mindful of the influences around you, you can create a supportive environment that nurtures your dreams and helps you achieve your full potential.

One important thing to remember on your journey is to be patient. Lots of people don't succeed, not because they're not strong enough, but because they can't wait. They want to see results right away, but the truth is, some things take time. You can't expect to achieve something in just a few days that really needs months or even years of work. Being patient doesn't mean just sitting around doing nothing. It means keeping at it, even when you can't see the payoff yet. It's about showing up every day, getting better, and quietly making progress. Lots of people give up just when they're about to make a breakthrough, simply because they get tired of waiting. But the ones who keep going, who keep pushing forward, are the ones who ultimately succeed. They're the ones who win. It's easy to get discouraged when you're not seeing the results you want right away. But the key is to keep moving forward, even when it feels like nothing is happening. Because the truth is, every step you take, every effort you make, is getting you closer to your goal. And if you can just be patient, and keep walking, you'll be amazed at what you can achieve. So don't give up, even when it gets tough. Just keep going, and trust that the breakthrough will come.

To make your journey easier, pick one thing that's really important to you and focus on it every day. This could be learning something new, getting better at a skill, building a career, starting a business, or creating content that people will love. A lot of people make the mistake of trying to do too many things at once, and then they get frustrated when nothing seems to be working out. But the truth is, success comes from concentrating on one thing and doing it over and over again. When you keep working at something, you start to get really good at it, and that's when things start to happen. It's like knocking on a door every day - eventually, someone is going to answer, and new opportunities will open up for you. So, don't try to knock on ten doors once in a while, just pick one and keep knocking until it opens. With time and practice, you'll become an expert, and doors will start opening naturally.

Don't let your past hold you back - it's what you make of it that matters. Your story, with all its ups and downs, can be a source of strength or a excuse for not trying. When you own your story, including the setbacks and failures, you take away its power to hurt you. But if you try to hide it, it can haunt you and hold you back. The thing is, getting to where you want to be isn't about having a perfect history - it's about creating a better future. So, don't be embarrassed about where you came from. Be proud of yourself for keeping going, for pushing forward, and for turning your story into a powerful tool for success. Remember, every step you take, no matter how small, is a step in the right direction. And that's something to be proud of.

Life is a journey and we all take different paths, but the steps to get there are always the same. First, you need to figure out where you're going, then you create a routine to help you get there. As you keep moving forward, you start to develop the skills you need, and eventually, you get to a point where you're doing things consistently. That's when the real growth happens, and before you know it, you start to see results. It's not that life gets easier, it's just that you become stronger and more capable of handling the tough stuff. If you stick to your path, success is pretty much guaranteed - not because things will always go smoothly, but because you'll be able to overcome any obstacles that come your way.

Don't worry if you're feeling left behind today. Remember, your journey is still ongoing. You're not running late, you're not failing, and you're definitely not weak. You're just taking things one step at a time. And the best part is, if you keep moving forward, you'll eventually look back and see that the tough road you're on right now is actually what made you stronger. It's the struggles you're facing that will help build your character and make you the person you're meant to be. So, don't give up, just keep walking.

The Day I Dropped Out

I was just going through the motions in my early teens, I was there, but I wasn't really living. School was a blur, my mind always wandering off to who-knows-where. It's not that I hated learning or anything, I just didn't get why it was such a big deal. Without a clear plan or goal, every day felt like Groundhog Day. I'd study every now and then, but most of the time I was just winging it, relying on luck and last-minute cramming to get by. Honestly, I wasn't building a future, I was just killing time, trying to survive from one day to the next.

The real problem wasn't that I was "not intelligent." The real problem was that I was confused, and confusion can look like laziness. I listened to people too much. One person would say, "This field is useless," and I would lose interest. Another would say, "You can't do that," and I would change my plan. I kept moving according to others' opinions like a leaf moved by the wind. When you don't know who you are, every voice sounds like truth. When you don't know where you are going, every road feels the same.

I just felt really unmotivated, you know. I didn't have anything to get me pumped up in the morning, no reason to think "today's the day I'm going to crush it". That spark was gone. I lacked discipline, and I didn't have a clear goal that felt achievable. Without discipline, even someone with a lot of talent can struggle. And without a clear vision, even the smartest person can lose their way. It's not about being talented or intelligent, it's about having a clear sense of purpose. That's where success really starts.

Then came the day I will never forget: my 10th grade result day.

I had a feeling something was off before it even happened. It wasn't because I had seen the grades or anything, but deep down, I knew I hadn't put in the work. I mean, I hadn't studied like I should have - I left everything until the last minute. I made excuses instead of actually doing the work. I was always thinking "maybe I'll get lucky" instead of "I have to do this." I remember those nights when I'd sit at my desk with my books open, but my mind would just wander off. I'd tell myself "I'll start studying tomorrow" and then tomorrow would come and I'd put it off again. The coursework felt overwhelming because I just didn't have a good grasp of the basics. And the fear was building up, you know? When you know you haven't done your part, you can't feel confident - you just feel like something bad is coming. It's like, when you're not prepared, you can't help but feel anxious. You start to think about all the things that could go wrong, and it's hard to shake off that feeling. I knew I had let myself down, and that was the hardest part to deal with. I had trusted in excuses and luck instead of actually putting in the effort, and now I was facing the consequences.

On result day, the air felt different. Even the silence felt loud. When I finally saw it, when it became reality, I felt like the ground disappeared under my feet.

I had failed.

In that moment, it wasn't just about passing or failing a test - it felt like my whole life was on the line, like everything I had worked for was crumbling down around me.

I walked into my house feeling really down, like I was carrying a heavy burden that I couldn't understand. My mouth felt dry, my hands were freezing, and my heart was beating super-fast, like it was trying to escape from something. When I told my dad what was going on, I was expecting him to yell or get really angry, but he didn't. He just got really quiet, like he was a million miles away, staring at something that I couldn't see. It was like he was looking into the future or something, and it was really weird. He just sat there, not saying a word, and it was freaking me out. I was used to him reacting in a certain way, but this silence was really unsettling. It was like he was trying to process everything, but I had no idea what was going on in his head.

That silence hurt more than anger.

Because in silence, you start imagining everything. You start hearing your own negative voice: "You disappointed him." You start feeling like you ruined everything. And when you already have no clear goals, failure doesn't just bring pain, it brings emptiness.

I hit rock bottom that day. Dark thoughts swirled in my head - not exactly plans, but a whole lot of negative emotions. I felt like my life was over, like I had no future, no career, nothing to look forward to. The shame was overwhelming, I felt stuck and hopeless, like I'd never be able to pick myself up. I was terrified that people would always see me as a failure, that I'd never be able to shake off that label. But here's the thing: if you've ever felt like life is just too much to handle, I want you to know that those feelings are real, but they don't have to stay. Talk to someone you trust, someone who can offer a listening ear and a helping hand. One conversation can be a game-changer, it can save you from years of pain and struggle. Don't be afraid to reach out, don't let those dark emotions consume you. You are not alone, and you are not defined by your failures. You can rise above them; you can find a way to heal and move forward.

I was stuck in a rut, feeling empty and lost. Every day was the same, I'd sit around, get up, walk around, and end up back where I started, with that same hollow feeling. I didn't want to hear it from anyone, no lectures, no advice, nothing. And as for hope, forget it - it just seemed like a cruel joke after what I'd just been through, a reminder of my failure.

Then I started going to the rooftop.

Not to run away. Not to do anything harmful. Just to breathe. Just to disappear from noise. I would lie down and look at the sky like the sky was the only place that didn't judge me. I did this again and again. One day became two. Two became a week. Almost two weeks passed like this—me staring at the sky, thinking about how a person can feel alive but feel finished at the same time.

And of course, people talked.

Some said it with fake sympathy: "We knew it."

Some people were brutally honest, telling me straight out: "You're not cut out for studying."

Some people just came out and said it: "This boy doesn't have what it takes."

Some people actually used my failure as a way to make themselves feel better about not trying hard enough, saying things like "See, not everyone can succeed" - it's like they were comforting themselves with my shortcomings.

When you are already down, people's words become louder. Their opinions start sounding like facts. And that is how many people stay defeated, not because they failed once, but because they believed what others concluded about them.

And that's when I heard the one voice that mattered most - my mom's.

One day, she sat down beside me, and it felt like I was under a protective umbrella, not being judged or criticized. She didn't launch into some long, drawn-out speech or try to make me feel bad about myself. Instead, she spoke to me in a gentle, soothing way, like a mother trying to comfort a child who's been hurt, her words a balm to my broken heart.

She whispered gently, "You are a Star, and you have the power to shine again."

That one sentence didn't fix everything, but it had a big impact. It allowed me to take a deep breath and feel okay again. I realized that just because I failed at something, it didn't mean I was a failure as a person. It reminded me that I'm still here, I'm still capable of doing things, and I can still make changes in my life. It's funny how one little sentence can make such a big difference, but it did - it gave me the permission to keep going, to keep trying, and to remember that one mistake isn't the end of the world.

My dad, who had been really quiet until then, finally said something that has stuck with me forever. He didn't try to make me feel better by pretending it wasn't a big deal, and he didn't try to make me feel worse by being too harsh. Instead, he just looked at me and said, "Don't give up on yourself just yet. One bad result doesn't define who you are or what you can do. Give yourself another shot, and don't let this one mistake decide your whole future."

It was then that I felt a tiny spark within the darkness, a small light that shone through.

Because when you fail, you don't only need motivation. You need someone to restore your self-belief.

That night, something shifted inside me. Not suddenly. Not dramatically. But genuinely.

I asked myself: "What if this failure is not my ending? What if it is my warning? What if it is my turning point?"

And for the first time, I didn't just feel regret—I felt responsibility.

I realized why I failed: I was directionless. I was inconsistent. I was listening to too many people and obeying too few principles. I was living without structure. I wanted results without routine. I wanted success without sacrifice.

I made a promise to myself, not to anyone else, it was a personal thing.

I will start again.

I will study again.

I will rebuild from scratch.

I will not let one chapter decide the whole story.

What motivated me wasn't just fear of failure. What motivated me was something stronger: the idea that I could still become someone my future self would be proud of. I imagined a life where I didn't carry shame. I imagined a life where my father's silence turned into pride. I imagined a life where my mother's words— "You are a Star. You can Rise Again. "—became true not because of luck, but because of effort.

That is how my comeback began.

It doesn't start with a flawless strategy or immediate self-assurance.

But with a decision:

I will give myself another chance.

So, I started thinking, what are the things that people do, the habits they have, and the ways they approach problems that can actually help them go from not doing well to doing really well?

I didn't just want to get by, I wanted to overcome and thrive, to find a way to "Rise Again" and make the most of every moment, to truly live.

The Hidden Years of Life

Before the doctorate, before the millions of views, before the applause, before the book titles and the stage, there was a version of me that almost nobody knew.

No cameras. No recognition. No crowds. No "success story."

Just a small flat in Sargodha City, and a young man trying to understand how to rebuild a life from the inside out.

People often meet you at your results and assume you were always strong. They see the final picture and forget the unfinished sketches. They see the light and never ask about the darkness. But every real success has a season that stays hidden, years that don't make headlines, days that don't get likes, nights that don't get applause.

Those were my hidden years.

I wasn't a famous influencer. I wasn't a popular author. I wasn't a speaker with an audience waiting for my words. I was just a person with a heavy past and a quiet dream, living far away from the spotlight, trying to build a future that didn't exist yet.

And that is what "hidden years" really are: when you are working on a life you cannot prove to anyone yet. When you have nothing in your hands except effort, and nothing in your heart except hope.

The hidden years are not glamorous. They are not cinematic. They are not "motivational" while you are living them. In those years, progress is slow, and doubts are loud. In those years, you are forced to face yourself, your laziness, your fear, your mood swings, your excuses, your weakness, your inconsistency. And you learn something important: the real enemy is not people outside you. The real enemy is the voice inside you that keeps asking, "What's the point?"

There were nights I couldn't sleep, not because I was enjoying life, but because my mind was busy with questions. "How will I fix my future?" "How will I become someone?" "How will I prove I'm not finished?" There were days when nothing looked like it was moving, but I kept moving anyway. There were times when I felt invisible, like I existed, but my existence didn't matter.

But I kept working.

I kept reading, learning, studying, thinking, and pushing myself. I kept writing when no one was waiting to read. I kept improving when no one was praising. I kept building discipline even when I didn't feel inspired.

Because I had one sentence in my mind—one rule that became my personal law:

Work while remaining silent until your success makes the noise.

That sentence saved me from distraction. It saved me from ego. It saved me from the need to announce my goals to people who didn't believe in me.

In the hidden years, I learned that talking about your plans can sometimes steal your energy, because you start enjoying the idea of success instead of doing the work of success. I learned that real builders are often quiet—not because they are weak, but because they are focused.

WHY HIDDEN YEARS MATTER

Hidden years are not wasted years. They are foundation years.

A tall building doesn't begin with the top floor. It begins underground. The stronger the foundation, the higher the building can stand. If the foundation is weak, the building may look beautiful, but it will not survive pressure.

That is what hidden years do: they build a foundation strong enough to carry success without collapsing.

These years taught me patience. They taught me consistency. They taught me how to work without immediate reward. They taught me how to survive without attention. They taught me that the greatest power in life is not fame; it is self-control.

Because success without self-control is dangerous. It can destroy you.

The hidden years trained me to become stable. They trained me to continue even when nothing "happened." They trained me to live beyond mood. They trained me to stay committed when motivation wasn't available.

And this is what many people don't understand: motivation is not the engine. Discipline is.

In the hidden years, discipline becomes your best friend.

A TRUTH ABOUT EVERY SUCCESSFUL PERSON

If you study the lives of great people, you will notice a pattern: every success has a silent season. A season when the world didn't know them. A season when they were ignored, underestimated, or forgotten.

Think of "Thomas Edison". People remember the light bulb, but they forget the thousands of failed attempts that came before it. Edison once said, "Genius is one percent inspiration and ninety-nine percent perspiration." That sentence is not just a quote. It is a description of hidden years, the sweat that nobody sees.

Or think about athletes who become champions. The world sees the trophy, but the trophy was built in empty gyms, early mornings, strict routines, and painful repetition. Success is always louder at the end, but it is always quieter in the beginning.

That is why hidden years are not something to be ashamed of. They are something to respect.

Because if you can learn to work in silence, you can build a success that lasts.

The biggest lesson the hidden years gave me.

The hidden years taught me how to stop listening to noise.

People will always have something to say. If you listen to them too much, you will never build your life, because their opinions change daily. One day they will encourage you, the next day they will discourage you. One day they will praise you, the next day they will doubt you.

So, I learned to stop living according to people's mouths.

I learned to live according to principles.

I stopped chasing quick results and started chasing correct habits. I stopped begging for motivation and started building routine. I stopped seeking validation and started seeking improvement.

In those years, I understood that you don't need the whole world to believe in you. You just need enough belief to take the next step.

And the next step.

And the next.

That is how hidden years become visible success.

The role of hidden years in my success.

When people later see your success, they think it happened "suddenly." But nothing good happens suddenly. The "sudden success" is usually the result of years of silent work.

When you see someone rise quickly, you are not seeing speed—you are seeing preparation.

My hidden years were preparation years. They shaped my mindset. They strengthened my discipline. They built my patience. They corrected my direction. They helped me grow into someone who could carry bigger responsibilities.

And this is why those hidden years are precious to me. Because they were not easy, but they were necessary. Without them, I might have achieved something—but I would not have become someone.

A MESSAGE FOR YOU

If you are in your hidden years right now—if you feel unseen, ignored, behind, or stuck—let me tell you something with full honesty:

You are not late.

You are not failing.

You are training.

You are building the foundation.

The work you do in silence will protect you in noise.

Keep going. Keep learning. Keep improving. Keep showing up. Even if the world doesn't clap. Even if nobody understands. Even if results are slow.

Because one day, when the time is right, your success will speak without you having to explain anything.

And when that day comes, you will look back and say the same words I say today:

I can't forget those hidden years of my life.

The Turning Point of my Life

People think a turning point is a dramatic moment—something loud, something public, something that happens in a single day. But I learned that the real turning points are often quiet. They begin inside you, long before the world sees any change. A turning point is not only a moment. It is a decision that becomes a direction—and then becomes a new life.

For me, the biggest turning point was understanding this truth: pain is not supposed to destroy you. Pain is supposed to build you—if you use it correctly. Pain should never become your weakness. Pain should become your fuel.

I believe pain can be one of the most motivational forces in the world. Not because pain is beautiful, but because pain is honest. Pain tells you, "Something must change." Pain pushes you when comfort makes you lazy. Pain wakes you up when excuses make you sleep. Pain creates urgency—and urgency creates movement.

The day I truly felt this was the day I stopped asking, "Why did this happen to me?" and started asking, "What will I do with this?" That question changed my life. Because a person who keeps asking "why" stays trapped in the past. But a person who asks "what now" begins building the future.

There was a time when I was deeply influenced by people's opinions. If someone praised me, I felt confident. If someone criticized me, I felt finished. My mood depended on their mouths. And that is a dangerous way to live, because people's opinions change like weather. Then one day I realized something that hit me like a slap of reality: If I keep living for people's approval, I will die without becoming myself. That was a turning point. I didn't become rude. I didn't become arrogant. I simply became focused. I stopped explaining my dreams to people who only understood limits. I stopped sharing my plans with negative voices who wanted me to stay small. I learned a powerful rule: not everyone deserves access to your vision. From that day, I made a decision: I will respect people—but I will not surrender my future to their opinions.

Excuses are comfortable, and comfort is a silent killer of potential. In the beginning, it's easy to blame circumstances, blame people, blame the system, blame time, blame luck. And sometimes circumstances are truly hard, life is not fair to everyone. But I learned something that changed me: even when life is unfair, responsibility is still your power. The moment I accepted responsibility, my life started moving. I stopped saying, "I can't," and started saying, "How can I?" I stopped waiting for motivation and started building discipline. I stopped dreaming only in my mind and started working with my hands. That was another turning point: I understood that success does not begin when life becomes easy. Success begins when you become serious.

Pain can either make you bitter or make you better. The difference is purpose. When I was hurt, rejected, underestimated, or ignored, I had two choices: to complain or to convert that pain into action. Slowly, I started choosing action. I started telling myself: "If this pain is real, then my effort must be real too." I began using pain like fuel. When I felt low, I worked. When I felt embarrassed, I improved. When I felt rejected, I came back stronger. I started treating pain as a message that said: "Build. Grow. Become." This is why I say pain can be motivational, because it can create a fire inside you that comfort can never create. Comfort makes you delay. Pain makes you decide.

Many people ruin their life waiting for the "perfect time." Perfect time is an illusion. The turning point happens when you realize that the right time is not found, it is created. I didn't rise because one day I felt perfect. I rose because one day I committed to routine. I started building small daily habits that looked ordinary but produced extraordinary results over time. I learned to value consistency more than excitement, because excitement is temporary but consistency is permanent. This is one of the biggest turning points anyone can have: when you stop living by mood and start living by discipline.

At some point, I realized that success is not something you chase outside. Success is something you build inside. Money can come and go. Fame can rise and fall. But the person you become, your mindset, your patience, your discipline, your ability to stand again, that stays with you forever. So, I stopped asking only for outcomes. I started working on identity. I began thinking like this: "If I become the right person, the right results will follow." That shift, from chasing success to becoming successful, was a turning point that changed everything.

During my growth, I spent time researching the lives of people who turned pain into power, because I wanted to understand what made them unstoppable. Two examples stayed with me deeply. The first is "The Imran Khan". When I studied his life, what shocked me was not only what he suffered, but what he became through that suffering. He did not allow pain to turn him into hate. He turned that hardship into strength, patience, leadership, and a bigger mission.

What I learned from him is that pain can either break your character, or build your character. The stronger you become inside, the more powerful your impact becomes outside. The second example is J.K. Rowling. When I read about her journey, I learned that her success was not born from ease. She faced intense struggle and repeated rejection before her work was accepted. What inspired me most was not just that she succeeded, but that she kept going when the world gave her reasons to stop. What I learned from her is simple: rejection does not mean you are wrong. Sometimes rejection means your time has not come yet, and your job is to keep improving until your time arrives.

A turning point can change everything because it changes the direction of your daily actions. Life is built in days, not in speeches. When you change what you do daily, you change what you become yearly. When you stop listening to negativity, your mind becomes lighter. When you choose responsibility, your future becomes clearer. When you turn pain into purpose, your struggle becomes meaningful. When you build routine, your results become inevitable. When you focus on becoming a better person, success becomes a natural outcome. That is what turning points do: they don't just change your mood; they change your identity.

Maybe your turning point will not look dramatic. Maybe it will be a quiet night where you finally decide, "Enough." Maybe it will be a morning where you wake up and say, "I will not live like this anymore." Maybe it will be a moment where you stop begging for motivation and start building discipline. Whatever your turning point is, remember this: You don't need a perfect past to build a powerful future. You don't need everyone to believe in you, you need to believe enough to begin. And you don't need a pain-free life, you need a purposeful life. Pain is not here to finish you. Pain is here to push you. And once you learn how to use it, you will realize the truth: A turning point is not something you wait for. A turning point is something you choose.

The Price of Consistency

Consistency is not a talent. It is a price.

Everyone loves the reward, but very few people respect the receipt. People celebrate the results of consistency, success, influence, respect, achievement, yet they rarely talk about what consistency quietly takes from you before it gives anything back. Because consistency does not take money first. It takes comfort. It takes ego. It takes sleep. It takes your weekends. It takes your excuses. It takes your old identity. And if you are not ready to pay that price, you will keep admiring other people's lives while living the same year again and again.

I learned this in my own journey, but not in a romantic way. I learned it in ordinary days, days that didn't feel special, days that didn't feel "motivational," days that didn't give quick results. The kind of days that decide your future, because your future is not built on your best days. Your future is built on the days when you feel nothing, yet you still do the work.

In my early struggle, I wasn't a known name. I wasn't a famous influencer. I wasn't an author people quoted. I wasn't a speaker with a crowd. I was just a man with a goal that looked too big for my current reality. I had small resources and big responsibilities. I had small results and big dreams. And I had to learn a rule that many people ignore: if you want a different life, you must be willing to live differently before the world agrees with you.

That is the first price of consistency: you become strange to normal people.

When you start being consistent, people don't always clap. Sometimes they question you. Sometimes they laugh. Sometimes they judge you. Sometimes they throw their doubts like stones. And you have to keep going anyway. Because consistency is not about proving something to people. Consistency is about building something inside yourself that no one can steal.

The second price of consistency is that it is boring. Consistency is not excitement. It is repetition. It is the same discipline, the same effort, the same commitment, again and again. It is waking up when your body says "sleep more." It is studying when your mind says "scroll." It is creating when your heart says "nobody cares." It is writing when you feel empty. It is practicing when there is no audience. It is showing up when you feel invisible.

This boredom is not punishment. It is training.

Most people want inspiration. Consistent people want improvement. Most people chase motivation. Consistent people build systems. That is why consistency looks simple from outside, but it is heavy on the inside. It is heavy because it requires you to win against yourself daily.

And there is another price that hurts even more: consistency delays reward.

When I was creating content in the early days, effort and reward did not match. I would write, record, edit, and post—and sometimes the response was silence. A few views. No comments. No encouragement. That silence tests you. It makes you feel like your work is disappearing into the air. It makes you question your value. It tempts you to stop.

But that is the real test: will you be consistent when the world is not watching?

Because the world only claps at the finish line. Consistency is the lonely road before the finish line exists.

The same is true for study, skill-building, and personal growth. In the beginning, consistency feels like sacrifice with no evidence. You study today, and life doesn't change tomorrow. You work hard this month, and the results may not show for months. This is where most people quit: not because they can't do it, but because they can't wait.

Consistency is the art of staying loyal to a future you cannot see yet.

I started understanding consistency like a law of life: small actions repeated daily become a force. Not because one action is powerful, but because repetition removes weakness. Repetition sharpens skill. Repetition builds identity. Repetition turns "I try" into "I am."

And identity is the real reward.

When you become consistent, you stop negotiating with yourself. You stop saying "maybe tomorrow." You stop making your mood the boss of your life. You become the kind of person who does what needs to be done. And that identity is priceless, because once you own it, it spreads into every area—study, business, relationships, health, faith, leadership, and influence.

This is why consistency is not only a habit. It is a lifestyle.

Think about great people who paid this price.

One example that always stands out to me is "Kobe Bryant". People loved the highlights, the trophies, the fame, but the real story was the unseen work. His greatness was not created on the match day. It was created in early mornings when the gym was empty, in practices when nobody was filming, in repetition that looked boring to outsiders. That is what consistency produces: the ability to perform under pressure because you have already done the work in private. The reward wasn't just skill, it was reliability. When the moment came, he could deliver, because he had paid the price when no one cared.

Another example I reflect on is "Imran Khan", because his journey shows what the price of consistency really looks like in real life. He has often shared the idea that a person who wants meaningful change must be ready to stay patient, keep showing up, and keep working even when progress is slow and the world is laughing. For years, he stayed committed to one mission, one message, and one struggle, and he kept paying the hidden price, criticism, setbacks, long delays, and loneliness, without quitting the road. The lesson I take from that is powerful: consistency is not about one big moment; it is about thousands of small moments where you refuse to stop. You pay for consistency with comfort, with ego, and with time, but if you keep paying that price, one day your reward becomes bigger than your struggle, and your results become louder than every doubt.

Now, when I look back at my own life, I can clearly see what I paid, and what I earned.

I paid with comfort. There were days when entertainment felt easier, but discipline mattered more. I paid with sleep, nights when I worked, studied, created, learned, and improved. I paid with ego, because consistency humiliates you before it honors you. You post and get few views. You try and fail. You start and feel small. Consistency forces you to accept being a beginner again and again, until you become a master.

I paid with social approval. When you stay consistent, people don't always understand you. Some will say you are wasting time. Some will say it's impossible. Some will say you are dreaming too big. Some will wait for you to fail so they can feel right. Consistency asks you to walk while carrying their doubts on your shoulders, and still keep your pace.

I paid with patience. Patience is expensive because it demands you to work without immediate reward. It demands you to plant seeds and trust the season. It demands you to stay committed even when nothing looks like it's growing.

And what did I earn?

I earned inner strength. I earned self-respect. I earned the ability to start, continue, and finish. I earned progress in education and growth in discipline. I earned influence that began from a small place and expanded through time. I earned a voice that people began to recognize because I did not stop when the numbers were small. I earned results that look "fast" to people, but were built slowly through hidden years.

Consistency gave me a life that inconsistency could never give.

Here is the most important truth: consistency is not about doing everything. It is about doing the right thing again and again. Many people stay busy but don't move forward. They do ten random actions and call it hard work. Consistency is different. It chooses a direction and commits to it. It builds one skill deeply. It repeats one discipline daily. It improves one weakness at a time. It turns scattered energy into focused power.

And consistency also teaches you a painful lesson: you can't keep the old life and expect a new future.

If you want success, you must sacrifice something. There is always a trade. The question is not "Will I sacrifice?" The question is "What will I sacrifice?" Because if you don't sacrifice for your dream, you will sacrifice your dream for comfort.

This is why the price of consistency is not only time. It is choice.

You choose discipline over distraction.

You choose routine over mood.

You choose long-term growth over short-term pleasure.

You choose progress over ego.

You choose action over excuses.

And slowly, those choices become your personality.

But here is the best part: once you pay the price long enough, consistency starts paying you back.

It pays you back in confidence, not fake confidence, but earned confidence. The kind that comes from knowing, "I can rely on myself." It pays you back in opportunities, because the world trusts people who show up. It pays you back in reputation, because consistency builds credibility. It pays you back in results, because effort compounds like interest. You may not see it day to day, but over months and years, it becomes unstoppable.

Many people misunderstand compounding. They think compounding is only money. But compounding is a law of effort too. One good day does not change your life. But one good day repeated becomes a new life.

That's why consistency is powerful: it makes your small actions heavy over time.

And that is why this chapter matters for you.

If you feel behind, don't search for a miracle, build a routine. If you feel weak, don't wait for motivation, build discipline. If you feel lost, don't keep switching directions, choose one path and walk it consistently. Even if you walk slowly, you will still reach far, because consistency turns slow movement into long distance.

If I could summarize the price of consistency in one sentence, it would be this:

Consistency will cost you what you want now, but it will reward you with what you want most.

So, ask yourself honestly: what is your price?

Are you willing to be bored sometimes?

Are you willing to work without applause?

Are you willing to stay consistent when results are slow?

Are you willing to be misunderstood while you are building?

Are you willing to sacrifice comfort to protect your future?

Because that is the difference between those who admire success and those who achieve it.

And if you can pay that price, quietly, daily, repeatedly, then one day your results will speak so loudly that you won't need to explain anything.

That is the reward of consistency.

And that is the reason I believe this: the future belongs to those who can keep going, even when it is hard, even when it is silent, even when it is slow.

Because consistency is not just the path to success.

Consistency is the proof that you deserve it.

The First Viral Moment

People see a viral video and think it happened in one night.

They see the views, the comments, the shares, the sudden attention—and they assume the creator got "lucky." They imagine one perfect idea, one perfect upload, and a life that changed instantly. What they don't see is the long road behind that moment. What they don't see is the invisible work, the quiet discipline, the repeated rejection, and the many times you stand up after nothing happens.

My first viral moment was not a miracle. It was a reward that arrived late, after a long season of silence.

In the beginning, I was recording content like someone talking to an empty room. I would think of an idea, write the message, record it, edit it, upload it, and wait. And sometimes nothing would come. No views, no response, no growth, just silence. You can't explain this kind of silence to someone who has never created something from zero. Because it isn't only about numbers; it becomes personal. You start questioning your voice. You start questioning your value. You start asking yourself, "Is my message worth anything? Does anyone even need what I'm saying?"

I wasn't making random content. I was working in a direction. I wanted to speak about life, relationships, struggle, failure, success, discipline, hope. I wanted to become a life coach and a voice people could trust. But the early stage of any journey is cruel because it forces you to work without proof. It forces you to do the right things while the world gives you no confirmation.

And still, I kept uploading.

I kept recording, editing, and posting. I kept improving my delivery. I kept learning how to speak with clarity, how to use emotion properly, how to say a big truth in simple words. I kept showing up, even when my mind tried to convince me that nothing was working.

Here is the truth that most people don't understand: you don't become viral by one video—you become viral by becoming better. And becoming better takes time, repetition, failure, and patience.

By the time my first big video went viral, I had already uploaded 783 videos. That number is not just a number to me. That number is a story.

It means 783 times I tried.

It means 783 times I showed up.

It means 783 times I faced the possibility of being ignored.

It means 783 times I improved, even when the results did not match the effort.

People see one viral clip and call it "overnight success." But what they are really seeing is 783 times of practice finally meeting the right moment.

Imagine a person tries something 783 times. Most people won't try 20 times. Many won't try 5 times. They try once, fail, and call it destiny. They try twice, feel embarrassed, and stop. They try a few times, don't get attention, and give up.

But if a person truly tries something 783 times, that person is no longer just "trying." That person is becoming. Becoming disciplined.

Becoming skilled. Becoming strong. Becoming patient. Becoming unstoppable.

Because there is something consistency does that is bigger than success: it changes your identity.

Now let me tell you about that first viral moment.

That video was about mother, about her value, her sacrifices, her love, and the way a mother becomes strength for a child even when the child feels weak. I didn't plan it like a "viral strategy." I didn't say, "This will get views." I said, "This is true, and people need to hear it." I spoke from emotion, from respect, from real feeling. And sometimes that is the secret of viral content: it is not perfect, it is real.

On the day it happened, I woke up like a normal day. Nothing felt different. I followed my routine, breakfast, daily tasks, the normal rhythm of life. I didn't wake up expecting a miracle. My mind was still living in the same world where effort often received silence.

Then I checked my phone.

And suddenly... it didn't feel like my phone. It felt like a storm.

Notifications were coming in like rain that didn't stop. Messages, comments, shares, new followers—one after another. I refreshed the screen, and the numbers kept climbing. At first, I thought it was a mistake. I thought maybe the app was glitching. Then I opened the video.

It was moving fast.

It reached three million views—and I still remember the feeling in my chest. It was not only happiness. It was shock, relief, and gratitude mixed together. It was like the universe finally said, "We saw you." It was like the invisible years suddenly became visible.

In that moment I felt something I had never felt before: the feeling of getting paid—not with money, but with proof.

Proof that my voice could reach people.

Proof that my message could matter.

Proof that I wasn't wasting my time.

Proof that the silence was not rejection—it was preparation.

And I won't lie: it felt like a reward for every time I felt ignored. It felt like a reward for every time I worked when no one cared. It felt like a reward for every moment I wanted to stop but didn't.

But the biggest thing that happened that day was not the views.

The biggest thing that happened was inside me:

I started believing on a new level.

Not the fake belief that comes from motivational quotes. The real belief that comes from experience. The belief that says, "If I can do it once, I can do it again. If I can reach people today, I can reach more tomorrow. If consistency brought me here, consistency can take me further."

That day taught me a deep lesson: sometimes life keeps you in silence not because you are rejected, but because you are being trained. Because if I had gone viral too early, before learning discipline, before learning patience, before learning how to handle pressure—I might have ruined myself with ego. I might have become proud. I might have become careless. I might have stopped improving.

But because the viral moment came after a long struggle, I respected it. I valued it. And I knew it was not the finish line. It was only a sign that I was finally on the right path.

This is something many people misunderstand about success: the first win is not the end. The first win is the test. It tests whether you become lazy after progress. It tests whether you become proud after attention. It tests whether you start chasing views instead of serving people.

That viral moment made me more responsible, not more relaxed. It made me more focused, not more distracted. Because I realized something: when people start listening, you cannot waste their time. You must deliver value. You must speak truth. You must keep improving.

And this is where I learned another powerful truth: viral is not luck alone, viral is preparation meeting timing.

You can't control timing fully, but you can control preparation.

Preparation means your message is clear.

Preparation means your delivery is improving.

Preparation means your consistency is strong.

Preparation means you understand people's emotions and needs.

Preparation means you keep showing up even when nothing happens.

That's why the "first viral moment" is not just a moment. It is a result of a long process.

And this is the journey people don't see: I went from 38 followers to more than 6 million followers by staying consistent, improving my message, and refusing to stop. Over time, I uploaded approximately 5,000 videos across different topics, relationships, struggle, failure, success, and life coaching, and I am still going on. Growth did not come because I got lucky once; growth came because I kept showing up, again and again, until people could not ignore the value anymore.

I remember studying the lives of successful people and noticing the same pattern. Many people become famous after years of being ignored. Many people win after years of losing. Many people get recognized after they have already paid the price quietly. Even in creative fields, writing, speaking, content creation, the world usually rewards the person who stayed longer than the person who quit early.

And when I looked at my own life, I saw the same message repeating itself: the reward is reserved for those who remain consistent when the reward is not visible.

If you take one lesson from my first viral moment, let it be this: don't judge your future by your early results. Early results are often weak because you are still learning. You are still building skill. You are still shaping your voice. But the person who keeps going becomes the person who grows.

This chapter also teaches you that rejection is not always real rejection. Sometimes it is just a delay. Sometimes it is a season where you are being strengthened. Sometimes it is life saying, "Not yet—improve more."

It teaches you that a single moment can change your life, but that moment usually arrives after a long period of invisible effort. That's why you must respect your small beginnings. Don't insult your small numbers. Don't feel ashamed of low views. Don't stop because the room is empty. Keep speaking. Keep building. Keep improving.

Because one day, the room won't be empty.

And when that day comes, you will understand what I understood when I saw those notifications and that video climbing into millions:

It was never just one video.

It was 783 times of standing up.

And if you can stand up that many times, success is not a question of "if."

Success becomes a question of "when."

From Rejection to Record Sales

When people look at success, they usually imagine a smooth road—talent recognized early, doors opening quickly, and support arriving on time. But my first book taught me something far more real: sometimes your biggest "yes" is hidden behind a long line of "no."

In 2021, I wrote my first book, "Listen, You Are a Star" and for me it wasn't just a manuscript. It was my story. It was pain converted into purpose. It was years of lessons, failures, restarts, and personal growth packed into pages. I believed in it like a person believes in a dream that kept them alive. And because I believed in it, I went to Lahore with hope in my heart and my book in my hands.

I met publisher after publisher. I walked into offices, sat across tables, and explained my message with sincerity. I told them, "This is not just a book. This is my life. This is my journey. Readers will connect with it. It will do good business." But most people didn't see what I saw. They didn't reject only the pages, they rejected the possibility. Some were polite, some were blunt, but the result felt the same: not interested. Not one or two. Many. Almost every publisher

I met gave me a version of the same answer: "It won't sell," "We can't invest," "It's risky," "We don't publish this type," "The market is tough."

Rejection has a special kind of pain. It doesn't only hurt your feelings—it attacks your confidence. It makes you doubt your own vision. And when rejection repeats, it becomes louder. It starts sounding like truth. You begin hearing it in your mind even when nobody is speaking. That is why rejection is so dangerous: not because people say no, but because you start saying no to yourself.

Still, I kept going.

And then one publishing company in Lahore, Nai Soch Publishers, finally agreed to publish—but with conditions that felt like another kind of rejection. They told me clearly: "We can print it, but we cannot invest in it. You will pay for printing, you will take the books with you, and book stores will not take your book for resale." In other words: they would print it, but they did not believe the market would carry it.

I remember sitting with that reality for a moment. Because this wasn't a small decision. This was a test of faith in myself. If I said yes, I would put my money on my message. I would take a risk that many people would call foolish. I would bring home thousands of copies of a book that everyone else was too afraid to invest in. And the fear was real: what if they were right? What if the books stayed in my home like silent boxes of disappointment?

But then I thought of something even heavier: what if I quit? What if I let fear decide my future? What if I accepted rejection as my destiny?

So, I said yes.

I paid for printing. And when the books arrived, I brought thousands of copies home. I still remember the feeling of those boxes, their weight, their presence, their quiet pressure. They were not just paper. They were a question sitting in my house: "Now what?" This was the moment where many people would panic. Many would lose confidence. Many would start blaming others. But in my heart, I knew something: if the market won't take my book, I will take my book to the people.

So, I went to my followers online and I spoke from the place that is strongest: truth. I didn't market it like a product. I presented it like a mission. I told them, in my own words and my own emotions: "This is not just a book. This is ten years of my life. If you want to read it, if you want to learn from my journey, click the link below."

That was it.

No big advertising budget. No bookstore support. No distribution network.

Just sincerity, a message, and the courage to ask.

And then something happened that I still remember like a movie scene: the next morning, I received "thousands of orders". Thousands. My screen kept lighting up nonstop, notifications, messages, order confirmations, payments, and people requesting delivery details, one after another, faster than I could process. In less than 24 hours, the books were gone. Sold out.

I was stunned, not because I didn't believe in the book, but because I saw how powerful direct connection with people can be when your message is real. I realized that sometimes the gatekeepers don't decide your fate. Sometimes your audience decides it. Sometimes the world that rejected you is simply not your real market.

When Nai Soch Publishers witnessed this, it became a turning moment for them too. I called them and said, "All books are sold out. I need more." That sentence is one of the sweetest sentences in a creator's life: I need more. Because it means the fear was wrong. The doubt was wrong. The rejection was wrong. And the story was still writing itself.

From there, the journey turned into momentum. This book didn't stay "one print." It became a movement in the market. It kept selling, kept reaching readers, kept spreading from hand to hand. Over time, it was reprinted more than 200 times, and over 200,000 hard copies were published. The demand kept growing. People began finding it online. More and more websites started listing it. The book became known as a record-selling book in Pakistan—something nobody predicted on those Lahore meetings when publishers were saying no.

The book was published in Urdu as "Suno Tum Sitare Ho", and later it was translated into English. And then, a beautiful thing happened that reminded me that a sincere message can cross borders: a lady from India, "Payal Maheshwari", reached out and said she had seen the book's success online, had read the English version, and wanted to translate it into Hindi as well. When you start from rejection and later your work travels internationally, you don't just feel proud—you feel humbled. You feel the weight of responsibility. You realize this isn't only about selling; it's about impact.

And that's the deeper truth: this story is not only about a book becoming successful. It is about a life lesson becoming visible.

Because what happened here was not magic. It was a set of principles.

One of the biggest principles is this: rejection does not always mean you are wrong. Sometimes rejection means the wrong people are judging the right work. Another principle is this: when doors don't open, build your own door. I didn't wait for bookstores to "accept" me. I went directly to the people. I didn't wait for big investment. I invested in myself. I didn't wait for someone to give me confidence. I proved my confidence through action.

A lot of people have powerful stories, but they never turn them into impact because they stop at rejection. They treat rejection like a stop sign. But rejection is often a test: "How badly do you believe in what you are doing?" If your belief collapses after one no, you weren't committed—you were only hoping.

And this is where I learned something else: support often comes after results, not before. Many people will doubt you while you are building, then praise you when you succeed. That is why you must learn to work without applause. If you depend on people's validation, you will never create anything meaningful. But if you depend on discipline, the results will eventually create the validation.

When I studied the lives of big authors, I saw this pattern everywhere. For example, Stephen King faced repeated rejection early in his career, and he even threw the manuscript of Carrie in the trash before it was rescued, revised, and later became the breakthrough that changed his life. I'm not comparing myself to his level—he is a global giant. But I relate to one part of that story deeply: the refusal to surrender. The willingness to keep walking with your work in your hands even when the world says, "Not interested." That mindset separates the dreamers from the doers.

And I also understand something that comes with influence: when your words reach people, you are not just entertaining them—you are shaping them. Today, I know my message is reaching millions, influencing the way people think, and helping them rebuild hope. I receive messages from people who say, "Your words changed my mindset," "Your content helped me survive a hard time," "I started again because of you." That is the real reward. Sales are numbers, but changed lives are legacy. And this is why I continue: to spread strength, love, and support—so people don't feel alone in their struggle.

The lesson is simple: rejection is not proof that you should stop— rejection is proof that you must become stronger. If your message is real, keep improving it, keep presenting it, and keep pushing it forward until it reaches the people it was meant for. Don't wait for permission. Don't wait for perfect support. Build your own way, speak to your audience directly, and let your results answer every doubt. Your story has value, but value needs courage to be delivered. If you have been rejected, it doesn't mean you are finished—it means you are being tested. Keep going. Keep working. Keep believing. Because one day, the same world that ignored your work will not only notice it—it will be forced to respect it.

From Dropout to Doctorate

Sometimes life takes you on a journey that feels like you're ending up right where you started, but as a different person. I had one of those moments on my graduation day at Governor House Karachi. I was all dressed up in my gown, holding my doctorate degree, and surrounded by people who seemed so confident and smart. But the whole time, I couldn't shake off this one thought that just kept repeating in my head: How did a high school dropout like me end up here? It was a pretty surreal experience. I mean, I was standing there, feeling like I didn't quite fit in with all these accomplished people, and yet, I had achieved something that I never thought I would. It was like my life had come full circle, and I was seeing everything from a completely new perspective. I guess that's what happens when you take a different path in life - you end up in unexpected places, but with a whole new understanding of yourself and the world around you.

I didn't succeed because I was the most intelligent person around. It wasn't because my life was simple or easy to navigate. And it certainly wasn't because I had everything I needed from the very beginning. The truth is, I learned how to get back up after I fell. I figured out how to start over when the weight of shame felt crushing, how to keep moving forward even when progress was slow and frustrating, and how to build a better future for myself, one small step at a time. It's a process that requires patience, perseverance, and a willingness to learn from your mistakes. By doing so, you can create a brighter tomorrow, even when today seems overwhelming.

I still remember the old version of me—the boy who failed in high school, the boy who felt directionless, the boy who heard people say, "Study isn't for you." Back then, my life didn't feel like a journey—it felt like a dead end. When you fail at the age when people are building their identity, failure doesn't stay on paper; it enters your self-image. You start thinking your failure is permanent. You start believing you are "that person." And the world around you helps that belief grow, because the world is quick to label.

But the truth is: the day you decide to change, the label starts losing power.

My journey back to education wasn't some big, dramatic moment. It didn't feel like a scene from a movie or anything like that. It was just a quiet decision I made to myself: I wasn't going to let one bad result define my whole future. That decision was like a seed that I planted, and then I had to nurture it every day with hard work, discipline, and perseverance. It wasn't easy, but I kept at it, day in and day out, and that's what helped me move forward.

Education is not only about books. It is about patience. It is about self-control. It is about learning how to delay comfort to protect your future. It is about doing the hard thing when nobody is forcing you. When I restarted, I wasn't competing with classmates. I was competing with my old self—my old habits, my old laziness, my old distractions, my old excuses. And that is the hardest competition, because the enemy lives inside you.

I've had those days when studying felt overwhelming, like I just wanted to give up. There were nights when the amount of work seemed like a huge mountain in front of me. Sometimes I even thought, "Maybe I'm not cut out for this." But then I realized something important: my own mind was going to challenge me before things started going my way. And if I could keep overcoming those challenges - the doubts, the laziness, the fear - then life would eventually start to fall into place and new opportunities would come my way.

Years later, I found myself standing at the Governor House in Karachi, but I wasn't just holding a piece of paper - I was holding something much more significant. It was proof that hitting rock bottom doesn't mean it's all over. Proof that starting again doesn't mean you've failed. It showed me that hard work and dedication can take you further than natural ability ever could. And most importantly, it proved that one bad experience doesn't define who you are as a person.

Something amazing happened next - my speech at graduation got seen by over a million people. This really got to me, because I knew it wasn't just being watched, it was actually touching people's hearts. It inspired those who were quietly struggling - students who hadn't done well, adults who felt left behind, and young people who had lost faith in themselves. When you see that your story is helping someone else, you start to understand that the tough times you went through were not a waste. They were actually getting you ready to make a difference.

So, what helped a high school dropout reach a doctorate?

I'd like to pass on ten down-to-earth rules that actually work - not just ideas or fantasies, but real principles that I've lived by. If you try out even a few of these, you'll likely see a big change in your life.

I stopped calling myself "a failure." Failing can be tough, it's not just about the exam, it's about how we see ourselves. I remember when I failed, it felt like I was failing as a person, not just the test. But then I realized, I am not my failure, I am a work in progress. I had to change the way I thought about myself, let go of the negative labels and focus on who I am and what I can achieve. It's like a weight is lifted off your shoulders when you stop defining yourself by your mistakes. Your self-image has to change before you can start to see real changes in your life. It's a simple idea, but it's not always easy to do.

I replaced motivation with routine. Motivation is emotional. Routine is practical. I didn't wait to "feel like studying." I built a structure. Same time, same place, same discipline. Even if the session was short, it was consistent. My routine became my rescue, because it protected me on days when I felt weak.

I picked up a valuable lesson, which is to begin with tiny steps, but to do something every single day.

When we fail, we often try to make up for it by setting huge goals for ourselves. We say things like, "I'll study all night, every night" or "I'll completely change my life in just one week." But then we end up burning out and giving up all over again. I've found that it's better to start small. Instead of trying to do too much at once, it's more effective to take tiny steps every day. For example, studying for just one hour each day can be more powerful than trying to cram ten hours of studying into just three days. The reason for this is that small daily steps are achievable, and achieving them helps to build our confidence. And when we have confidence, we start to believe in ourselves.

I learned for my own benefit, not to show off to others.

At first, I was all about getting quick results - I wanted to pass with flying colors, show everyone what I could do, and prove them wrong. But as I went along, I realized that to really get ahead, I needed to dig deeper. So, I stopped focusing on just getting good grades and started studying to really master the subject. When you study to understand something, rather than just memorize it, you retain it forever. And that's when learning becomes truly powerful.

I made a decision to tune out the negative voices and stop arguing with myself about my fate.

You don't have to convince everyone around you that your goals are worth pursuing. Sometimes, people's skepticism has nothing to do with you, but rather their own limitations and fears. I've learned to be more mindful of who I share my aspirations with, not because I'm being rude, but because I'm being intentional. My dreams don't require a consensus - they require my dedication and hard work every single day. I've come to realize that it's okay to be selective about who I confide in, and that's not being disrespectful, it's being focused. When you're trying to move forward, you don't need everyone's approval, you just need to keep moving forward, one step at a time.

I built self-accountability like a discipline. I took a step back and stopped making excuses. Even when things got tough, I asked myself: What can I take charge of right now? I started keeping track of my daily habits - what I was learning, what I was finishing, what I was putting off, and what I was skipping. Being accountable isn't always easy, but it's the most genuine way to improve. When you start taking responsibility, you stop pretending everything is okay when it's not. You begin to see things as they really are, and that's when real growth happens.

I learned to manage energy, not just time. Some days I had time but no energy. Some days I had energy but no direction. I learned that success requires both. I improved sleep where possible, protected my mind from useless stress, avoided people who drained me, and built simple habits that gave me strength. When your body and mind cooperate, your efforts multiply.

I used my pain as fuel, not as a wound. Pain can have two effects on us - it can either make us bitter or make us better. I've always chosen the latter, and I've done so repeatedly. Each time I recalled my past failures, I didn't let them drag me down; instead, I used them as a driving force, telling myself, "I will prove to myself that I can overcome this." My pain became a reminder to keep pushing forward, not a reason to give up. This mindset shift is a crucial strategy that has helped me navigate life's challenges.

I made it a point to always be consistent, even when it seemed like no one was paying attention.

There is a stage where you are improving, but the world still can't see it. This stage is dangerous because it feels like nothing is happening. But that stage is where real winners are formed. I kept going. I kept showing up. I kept building. Because I learned: your future is being built in your invisible days.

I turned my story into a mission bigger than myself. Having a goal that's just about you, like getting rich or famous, can make you lose interest fast. But when you're working towards something that helps others, you get a boost of energy. I wanted my journey to count for something more. I wanted my story to inspire people who feel like they're falling behind. Having that mission gave me the patience to keep going. It gave me the courage to face challenges. And it gave me a reason to keep pushing forward, even when things got tough.

Looking back, I can see that getting my doctorate wasn't the biggest deal. What really mattered was how I thought about things, how I kept going even when life got tough. That's what really got me through. The doctorate was just the end result. The real accomplishment was who I became along the way - someone who is disciplined, consistent, responsible, and focused. I learned a lot about myself and how to stay on track, even when things got rough. It's funny, because now I realize that it wasn't just about achieving a goal, but about becoming a better person in the process.

When I stood on that stage, degree in hand, I didn't feel superior to others. Instead, I thought about how far I'd come since my lowest point. And that's what made my message so impactful - it was a reminder that anyone can turn their life around, no matter what they're going through. People don't just need to be told what to do, they need to believe that they can actually do it. They need to see that it's possible to bounce back from failure, and that's what gives them hope. My speech resonated with so many because it showed them that a comeback is within reach, and that's a powerful thing.

Here's the thing: what happened in the past doesn't get to decide what's going to happen in the future. You can learn from your mistakes, but you don't have to be controlled by them. Failure can actually be a good teacher, if you're willing to listen. The key is to be brave, to start again, to be humble and learn from what went wrong, and to keep going, consistently, until you get it right.

Starting over can be tough, but it's a lot easier when you're honest with yourself. Just say, "I'll start again" and mean it. You don't have to be perfect; you just have to be strong enough to keep going every day. And then, one day, you'll look back and see how far you've come - you'll have achieved your goals, you'll be respected, and your life will be totally different. I know how that feels, I've been there myself, like when I was at the Governor House in Karachi, and I whispered to myself...

I was never finished. I was only becoming.

CORE SUCCESS FOUNDATIONS

The Philosophy of Success

Success is one of the most used words in the world, and also one of the most misunderstood. Everyone wants it, everyone talks about it, and yet most people chase it without knowing what it truly is. They run fast, but they don't ask where they are going. They sacrifice years, but they don't ask what they are becoming. They achieve something, yet they still feel empty—because they reached a destination that was never their real dream.

So, before we talk about how to succeed, we must answer one important question:

What is success?

Is success good health?

Is it millions of dollars?

Is it a big house?

Is it inner peace?

Is it a beautiful family?

Is it fame and recognition?

The honest answer is: success is not one thing. Success is a balance. It is a life that is progressing on the outside and stable on the inside. It is achievement with meaning. It is growth with peace. It is discipline with dignity.

Money matters—because money gives options, security, and comfort. But money alone is not success. I have seen people with money but no sleep, money but no respect, money but no relationships, money but no peace. Money is a tool. It is not a destination.

Fame also matters in a world where influence can spread ideas and help people. But fame alone is not success. Many famous people are lonely. Many are anxious. Many are trapped in the fear of losing attention. Fame is powerful, but it is also dangerous when it becomes your identity.

A big house can be a blessing—but a big house without a calm mind feels like a beautiful prison. Good health can be a gift—but health without purpose becomes a comfortable emptiness. A beautiful family is a treasure, but family without love and respect becomes a burden. Even inner peace, if it becomes laziness—can turn into stagnation.

So, what is the real philosophy of success?

Success is becoming.

Becoming disciplined.

Becoming responsible.

Becoming emotionally strong.

Becoming useful.

Becoming a person whose life moves forward with meaning.

A truly successful person is not someone who has everything. A truly successful person is someone who knows what matters, and builds a life around it.

SUCCESS IS NOT A TROPHY, IT IS A LIFESTYLE

Many people think success is a moment. But success is not a moment. It is the result of many small choices repeated daily. A person who wins once is not necessarily successful. A person who can repeat excellence, day after day, year after year, has built success as a lifestyle.

Success is not only what you achieve. It is also what you refuse. You refuse laziness. You refuse excuses. You refuse being controlled by fear. You refuse wasting time. You refuse living without a goal. You refuse becoming a slave to people's opinions.

This is why success begins internally.

If your mind is weak, your life will be weak.

If your habits are careless, your future will be careless.

If your discipline is inconsistent, your results will be inconsistent.

This is the philosophy: your life becomes your habits.

In my understanding, real success stands on five pillars. If one pillar is missing, life may look successful from outside, but it will feel unstable inside.

Success requires a clear direction. Without direction, you will be busy but lost. Many people are working hard, but they are working on the wrong things. A successful person knows what they want, why they want it, and what they must do daily to reach it.

Discipline is the bridge between dreams and reality. Without discipline, dreams remain fantasies. Discipline means doing the right thing even when you don't feel like it. It means routine. It means consistency. It means self-control.

Success is not only personal. It is also relational. A person with achievements but broken relationships is not truly successful. The best success is one that does not destroy your family, your character, your respect, and your humanity. Real success includes love, loyalty, respect, and good manners.

Your body is your vehicle. Without health, your achievements become heavy. Success without health is like building a palace on weak foundations. You may stand tall today, but you will suffer tomorrow. Good sleep, movement, and basic self-care are not luxury—they are strategy.

Inner peace is not laziness. Inner peace is emotional stability. It means your mind is not constantly burning in worry. It means you can face pressure without losing yourself. It means you can work hard without becoming hateful, arrogant, or broken. Inner peace is what makes success enjoyable.

Now ask yourself honestly: if you have money but no peace, are you successful? If you have fame but no family love, are you successful? If you have a big house but no health, are you successful?

The philosophy of success is not choosing one and ignoring the rest. It is building balance.

Why many people chase the wrong success?

Many people chase success to impress others. They want a car to prove something. They want a title to silence critics. They want money to feel superior. They want fame to feel important.

But success built on ego becomes pressure. You will always feel you must prove yourself again and again. You will never feel enough. And one day you will realize: you built a life for people who don't truly care.

That is why the first step is purity of intention: build success for growth, for meaning, for contribution—not only for showing off.

SUCCESS IS ALSO CONTRIBUTION

One of the deepest definitions of success is usefulness. How many people became better because you existed? How many hearts became stronger because of your words? How many lives became hopeful because of your presence?

This is something I learned personally as my voice reached people. When I started receiving messages like, "Your words changed my mindset," "Your content helped me during depression," "I started again because I listened to you," I realized success is not only about personal victory. Success is also about impact. It is about using what you learned in your struggle to lift someone else out of theirs.

A person can be rich and still useless.

A person can be famous and still empty.

But a person who adds value becomes successful in a way the world can't cancel.

Abdul Sattar Edhi. He was not famous for luxury, but he became respected globally because he lived for service. He built a legacy not through big houses, but through big heart. His success was contribution and humanity. That is why people remember him with love. This teaches us that success is not only what you own; it is what you give.

Another example is Cristiano Ronaldo. People see the trophies and the money, but behind that is extreme discipline. His success is not accidental. It is built through routine, training, focus, and hunger to improve. This teaches us that success is not only dreaming; it is daily work. You can't wish your way into success, you must work your way into it.

These examples show two sides of success: contribution and discipline. Both matters.

I want to share one small truth: when I moved from being unknown to being heard, I realized success is not only reaching people—it is staying worthy of their trust. Influence is not success if your character is weak. Achievement is not success if your habits are broken. That is why I always remind myself: results can make noise, but character is what keeps the respect.

So, what is success?

Success is waking up without regret, because you are living with purpose.

Success is progress with peace.

Success is growth without losing your values.

Success is being disciplined enough to build your future and humble enough to keep learning.

Success is health that supports your dreams, relationships that support your heart, and a mission that gives meaning to your struggle.

You can have millions and still feel poor if your mind is broken.

You can have fame and still feel invisible if your heart is empty.

You can have a big house and still feel homeless if your home has no love.

That is why the philosophy of success is simple:

Build a life that is strong on the inside and progressing on the outside.

If you want to be successful, don't chase success first. Chase clarity. Chase discipline. Chase skill. Chase good habits. Chase emotional strength. Chase values. Chase usefulness.

Because when you build the right person, the right results will follow.

And when you reach them, you won't only look successful.

You will feel successful.

The Dream of Success

A dream is not a decoration for the mind. A dream is a direction for the life.

Many people carry dreams, but their dreams are weak—not because the dreams are small, but because the dreams are unclear. They say, "I want success," but they can't explain what success looks like in their own life. They say, "I want a better future," but they don't know what "better" means. They say, "I want to change," but they don't know what they want to change into.

And because the dream is unclear, their effort becomes confused. They start, stop, restart, and repeat the same cycle. They work hard sometimes, then disappear. They get motivated one day, then fall into old habits the next day. Their life becomes a collection of good intentions without a clear destination.

That is why the dream of success is not only about wanting something. It is about seeing something clearly enough that it pulls you forward.

A real dream has three qualities: it is personal, it is meaningful, and it is specific.

A personal dream is not borrowed from society. It is not copied from a friend. It is not forced by family pressure. It is something that fits your nature, your values, and your deeper calling. A meaningful dream is not based only on ego; it includes purpose. It includes contribution. It includes becoming someone you respect. A specific dream is not a vague wish; it has shape. You can describe it. You can measure it. You can build a plan around it.

Most people fail because they never upgrade their dream from a wish to a vision.

A wish says: "I hope life becomes better."

A vision says: "I will build a better life, and I know how it will look."

The first mistake is thinking dreams are only for the lucky or the gifted. They think, "Dreaming is fine, but not for me." They look at their background, their failures, their finances, their education, their age, and they conclude that dreaming is dangerous.

But the truth is: dreaming is not dangerous. Living without a dream is dangerous. Because when you have no dream, you become easy to control. People's opinions control you. Your emotions control you. Your circumstances control you. Even your distractions control you. Without a dream, you don't direct your life—you drift.

A dream is not a guarantee you will succeed. A dream is a guarantee you will not remain stuck.

The second mistake: dreaming without paying the price. Many people want the results of a dream without the discipline of a dream. They want success but not sacrifice. They want progress but not pain. They want a changed life but not changed habits.

But dreams are expensive. Not expensive in money first— expensive in discipline.

A dream demands:
time you used to waste,
habits you used to enjoy,
friends you used to follow,
comfort you used to protect.

Every dream comes with a receipt. And if you don't pay the price early, you will pay regret later.

The third mistake: dreams that are too big but too fragile. Some people dream big, but their dream breaks after small problems. One criticism, and they stop. One failure, and they quit. One delay, and they lose hope.

That means the dream was not weak—the belief was weak.

A dream needs roots. Roots are built by patience, routines, and deep reasons. If your dream has no strong reason, it becomes fragile. If your dream has a strong reason, it becomes unbreakable.

So, ask yourself: Why do you want success?

If your reason is only to impress people, you will quit when they don't clap.

If your reason is to escape pain, you will quit when you feel pain.

But if your reason is to grow, to build, to contribute, to honor your potential—then no obstacle can stop you.

THE DREAM BEGINS WITH IDENTITY

The dream of success starts when you stop seeing yourself as a victim and start seeing yourself as a builder. A victim says, "Life happened to me." A builder says, "I will build something from what happened to me."

This shift is powerful, because your dream is not only a destination—it is a new identity.

When I started rebuilding my own life, the dream was not "a degree" or "views" or "recognition." The dream was deeper: I wanted to become a person who could rise after falling. I wanted to become disciplined. I wanted to become someone who could finish what he starts. Because I realized: if I become strong inside, I can create a strong life outside.

That is where real dreams are born—inside character.

The blueprint of a real dream. A real dream is not one sentence. It is a blueprint. And a blueprint has layers.

The first layer is who you want to become. Not what you want to get—who you want to become. For example: disciplined, educated, skillful, respected, calm, confident, healthy, useful.

The second layer is what you want to build. For example: a career, a business, a platform, a family life, a body of work, a stable income, a home.

The third layer is why it matters. This is the fuel. A dream without "why" becomes weak. A dream with "why" becomes unstoppable.

When you build these three layers, your dream stops being emotional and starts becoming practical.

DREAMS NEED DEADLINES, BUT FLEXIBLE ONES

Some people don't set deadlines because they fear disappointment. They say, "If I set a target and I fail, I will feel bad." So they stay vague. But vagueness is the enemy of success.

A dream without deadlines becomes a fantasy. Not because deadlines are magic, but because deadlines create urgency.

However, deadlines should be flexible, not fragile. If you fail to reach a goal by a certain date, it doesn't mean you failed. It means you adjust the plan and continue. The dream remains. Only the timeline changes.

DREAMS SURVIVE THROUGH SYSTEMS

The biggest secret of successful dreamers is that they don't rely on feelings. They build systems.

A system is a set of daily actions that move you forward even when you don't feel like it. A system protects the dream in difficult seasons.

For example:

If your dream is education, your system is daily study hours,

If your dream is health, your system is daily movement and clean eating,

If your dream is influence, your system is daily creation and learning.

Your dream is only as strong as the system you build around it.

THE DREAM MUST INCLUDE FAILURE

Most people fear failure because they think failure is the opposite of success. But failure is not the opposite of success. Failure is often part of success.

A dream that includes failure becomes realistic. A dream that ignores failure becomes fragile.

When you dream, don't ask, "What if I fail?" Ask, "What will I do when I fail?" Because failure is not a question—it is a season. The question is whether you will quit or learn.

A real dreamer does not fear failure. A real dreamer fears stagnation.

THE DREAM MUST BE PROTECTED FROM DISTRACTIONS

Distractions are not always bad things. Sometimes distractions are comfortable things. Sometimes distractions are small pleasures that slowly steal your life.

The dream of success requires you to say "no" to many things that feel good now so you can say "yes" to a life that feels good later.

That is the hard part of dreams: they demand delayed gratification. But delayed gratification is the fingerprint of greatness.

We have example of "Walt Disney". People see Disney as a symbol of imagination and success, but behind it was a dream that faced rejection and setbacks. His dream was larger than his circumstances, and he kept rebuilding until the dream became an empire. The lesson: a dream may be delayed, but it is not denied if you keep building.

Another example is "Muhammad Ali". Beyond boxing, his dream was identity. He believed in himself before the world believed in him. He spoke his dream out loud and then paid the price through discipline and sacrifice. The lesson: belief is not arrogance when it is backed by effort.

These examples teach something important: big dreams are not achieved by big wishes. They are achieved by big endurance.

A MESSAGE TO THE READER

If your life feels stuck, it may not be because you lack talent. It may be because you lack a clear dream that pulls you. You may be waking up daily and spending energy, but without a destination your energy becomes waste.

So, build your dream properly. Write it. Describe it. Make it specific. Make it meaningful. Tie it to purpose. Create a system around it. Protect it from distractions. Expect failure. Stay consistent. Keep adjusting.

Because the dream of success is not a fairy tale. It is a life plan.

And the day your dream becomes clear, something powerful happens: your excuses become weaker, your discipline becomes stronger, and your life begins to move.

Not because life becomes easy—because your direction becomes real.

That is the dream of success.

And if you protect it, it will one day protect you.

The Belief in Success

There's a big difference between wanting to be successful and really believing you can be. Wanting something is all about how you feel, it's emotional. But believing in something is deeper, it's about being sure of it, no matter what. When you want something, your feelings can change from one day to another, but when you believe in something, it stays with you even when things get tough. Lots of people want a better life, but they don't really think they can make it happen - and that's why they give up too soon, put things off, or just quit without making a noise.

Belief isn't just about being motivated by a sentence or two. It's about making a decision deep down that says, "I'm going to find a way, no matter what it takes." This kind of belief isn't about being blindly confident, but rather about having confidence that's built on real things - like small victories, daily habits, and keeping your commitments over and over again. It's what helps you keep moving forward, even when you can't see where you're going yet. You just know you'll get there, and that's what keeps you going.

When you look at people who have achieved success, one thing stands out: it's not that they have the best resources at their disposal, but rather that they have an unshakeable belief in themselves. This belief is a powerful force that influences every aspect of their lives, from their thought process to the way they communicate, the challenges they take on, and the things they choose to accept or reject. It's what drives them to push beyond their limits and strive for excellence, even when the odds are against them. Essentially, their strong belief system becomes the foundation upon which they build their success, and it's what sets them apart from others.

Because belief is not only what you feel. Belief is what you act on.

THE REAL MEANING OF BELIEF

Many people confuse belief with positivity. They think belief means always feeling strong, always feeling confident, always feeling hopeful. That is not belief. That is emotion.

Belief means you will still move forward even when you feel afraid. Belief means you will still do the work even when your mind is tired. Belief means you will still take action even when your heart is uncertain. Belief means you don't need perfect confidence—you need enough faith to take the next step.

A person without belief delays action.

A person with belief creates action.

So, having faith in your ability to succeed isn't just something you think about, it's actually something you get used to doing over time, it becomes a part of who you are.

WHY PEOPLE LOSE BELIEF

People lose belief for many reasons, but the most common reason is this: they judge their future by their past. If they failed before, they assume they will fail again. If they were rejected, they assume they will always be rejected. If they were ignored, they assume their voice doesn't matter.

This is one of the biggest lies the mind tells you: "Because it happened before, it will happen again."

But the future is not controlled by your past. It is controlled by your choices today.

Another reason people lose belief is because they listen to the wrong voices. Many voices speak from fear, not from wisdom. Some people discourage you because they don't understand your vision. Some discourage you because they are jealous. Some discourage you because your growth reminds them of their own laziness. And if you allow those voices to enter your heart, belief becomes weak.

Another thing to consider is that people often want to see instant results. But when things don't happen right away, they start to think that nothing is going to change. What they're forgetting is that real progress takes time - it's not something that happens overnight. It's like planting a seed - you don't see it growing, but it's developing slowly, quietly, under the surface. And at the start of anything new, it's always a bit slow going - that's just the way it is.

Believing in something can stay strong when you realize one important thing: just because something is delayed, doesn't mean it's not going to happen.

BELIEF IS BUILT, NOT FOUND

A powerful belief is not found like a lucky coin. It is built like a building.

It's constructed in three main parts: what we tell ourselves, the facts we gather, and the world around us.

Self-talk is the language you use inside your head. Many people destroy their belief without realizing it. They say things like, "I'm not smart," "I can't do it," "I always fail," "I'm too late," "I'm not capable." These sentences become identity.

Belief begins when you change the script. Not by lying to yourself, but by speaking growth into yourself. Instead of "I can't," you say, "I'm learning." Instead of "I always fail," you say, "I failed before, but I can improve." Instead of "I'm not capable," you say, "I can become capable through effort."

Words shape perception. Perception shapes action. Action shapes results.

Evidence is the second stage. Belief becomes strong when you collect proof. And proof does not have to be big. Even small progress is proof. One hour of study is proof you can be disciplined. One completed task is proof you can finish. One healthy habit is proof you can change. One honest conversation is proof you can grow.

Most people wait for belief before action. But belief often comes after action. You take a step, then your heart becomes stronger. You do the work, then you gain confidence. You face fear, then you build courage. This is why consistent action is one of the greatest builders of belief.

Environment is the third stage. Your environment is not only your place—it is your people, your content, your routine, your daily inputs.

If you are surrounded by negativity, belief will struggle to survive. If your mind is consuming useless content, belief will become lazy. If your circle is full of dream-killers, your vision will start shrinking.

Belief needs protection. The way a flame needs wind control, belief needs environment control.

THE BELIEF TEST: WHAT YOU DO WHEN NOBODY IS WATCHING

The deepest form of belief is what you do in private. Because belief is not proven by words—it is proven by consistency. If you truly believe in success, you will build habits that match that belief.

This is why many people are confused: they say they believe, but their habits deny their belief. They say they want success, but they don't study. They say they want growth, but they waste time. They say they want a new life, but they repeat the old routine.

Belief is not what you say. Belief is what you practice.

If you practice excuses, you believe in failure.

If you practice discipline, you believe in success.

BELIEF IS ALSO REALISM

Belief is not pretending the road is easy. Belief is accepting the road is hard—and walking anyway.

Real belief says: "I will face obstacles, but I will not stop."

Real belief says: "I will fail sometimes, but I will learn."

Real belief says: "I will be rejected sometimes, but I will improve."

Real belief says: "I will be late sometimes, but I will continue."

Belief becomes dangerous only when it becomes arrogance. Belief should not make you careless. Belief should make you serious. It should make you humble enough to learn and strong enough to continue.

A TRUTH FROM MY LIFE

There have been times in my life when all I had was my belief. When it seemed like nobody noticed me, when progress was slow, and when my hard work didn't pay off, I had to hold on to my belief like it was a lifeline. It wasn't that I always felt confident, but I just couldn't accept that giving up was a permanent solution. I realized that belief can be a quiet thing - it doesn't have to be loud or flashy. Sometimes, it just means keeping going, even when things seem tough. It's about persevering, even when it feels like nobody is watching, and even when progress is slow. For me, belief has been a powerful tool that has helped me get through the tough times, and it's something that I've learned to rely on, even when everything else seems uncertain.

I figured something out - when you consistently show up and follow through, your belief in yourself grows stronger. This happens because your actions start to prove to your own mind that you're capable and not weak. As you stick to your routine, it becomes evidence that helps convince your mind to stop doubting you.

TWO EXAMPLES OF BELIEF IN SUCCESS

Take "Oprah Winfrey", for instance. She had to overcome some huge challenges when she was younger, but she never gave up on herself. She always believed she could do more, and that belief really drove her to succeed. It's like her background could have held her back, but she didn't let it define her. Instead, her belief in herself became this powerful force that shaped who she is, what she does, and the difference she's made in the world.

Take "Michael Jordan", for instance. Getting cut from his high school basketball team could have easily defined him, but he didn't let it. Instead, he used it as a catalyst to push himself harder. Through relentless training and self-improvement, he came back stronger and more determined than ever. What's interesting is that his success wasn't just about feeling confident or believing in himself - it was about putting in the work and discipline to make his vision a reality. He repeated this process over and over until his talent and dedication couldn't be ignored, and the world was forced to take notice.

These stories teach a simple lesson: belief does not remove hardship. Belief gives you power to rise through hardship.

HOW TO BUILD BELIEF IN YOUR OWN LIFE

Start by choosing one area where you want success—education, business, health, relationships, or influence. Then build belief through small daily proof.

Start small, be consistent. Keep your daily promises to yourself, and you'll begin to trust yourself more. As you do, your confidence will grow, and so will your motivation. With increased motivation, you'll put in more effort, and that's when you'll start to see real progress. It's a simple but powerful cycle: promise, belief, effort, results. By sticking to your routine, no matter how small, you'll build momentum and set yourself up for success.

Also, stop giving your mind negative evidence. If you keep quitting, your mind learns: "We don't finish." If you keep delaying, your mind learns: "We don't act." If you keep wasting time, your mind learns: "We don't build." So, give your mind a new identity by behaving like the person you want to become.

And finally: be patient with the process. Belief is not built in one speech. It is built in repeated effort. The strongest belief is the one that survives slow seasons.

FINAL LESSON

Belief in success is not a gift for special people. It is a skill for serious people.

When you build belief, you stop living as a reaction to life. You start living as a creator of life. You stop being controlled by the past. You start building the future.

And this is the deepest truth:

Success belongs to the person who believes long enough to stay consistent, until belief becomes reality.

Determine the Direction

Many individuals don't fail due to a lack of strength, but rather because they lack a clear sense of direction. They possess energy, talent, and dreams, yet they don't know where they're headed. As a result, their life becomes a hectic journey without a destination. They try their hand at various things, start numerous plans, and discuss several goals, but after a while, they feel exhausted, perplexed, and disheartened. This is because moving without direction isn't progress - it's just a lot of noise. Without a clear path to follow, all their efforts are essentially pointless, leaving them feeling unfulfilled and uncertain about their future. Having direction is what gives life meaning and purpose, and without it, people can feel lost and disconnected from their goals. It's the difference between making progress and just going through the motions.

Having a sense of direction is really powerful. It means you're not just floating around, letting things happen to you. You're in control, like a ship with a compass, navigating through life. You might still hit some rough patches, but you'll always know where you're headed. It's like being the captain of your own ship, making your own decisions, and not letting others dictate your path. When you know your direction, you're not swayed by what others think or by the latest trends. You're focused on your goals and you keep moving forward, no matter what. It's a great feeling, being in charge of your own life and knowing where you're going.

Determining direction is a big deal, it's not something you can just take lightly, it's a choice that can affect your whole life.

The difference between a goal and a direction

A goal is a target. Direction is a way of living.

A goal might be: "I want to earn money."

A direction might be: "I want to build a skill and a career that creates stable income."

A goal might be: "I want to be famous."

A direction might be: "I want to become a voice that adds value and influences people positively."

A goal might be: "I want to be fit."

A direction might be: "I want to live with health, discipline, and energy."

Goals can change. Direction should remain stable.

When people don't have direction, they chase random goals. They change their mind every week. They waste years switching paths. And then they blame "luck" or "life." But the truth is, life rewards focus.

DIRECTION STARTS WITH TRUTH

To determine direction, you must face truth. Not the truth people want to hear, but the truth you need to accept.

Truth about your strengths.

Truth about your weaknesses.

Truth about what you enjoy.

Truth about what you avoid.

Truth about your responsibilities.

Truth about your environment.

Truth about your priorities.

Many people choose direction based on fantasy. They choose what looks exciting, what looks easy, what looks glamorous. But real direction is chosen based on honesty.

A strong direction does not begin with "What will people say?"

A strong direction begins with "What do I truly want to build, and what can I realistically commit to?"

THE MOST DANGEROUS LIFE IS A DIRECTIONLESS LIFE

A directionless life is dangerous because it becomes reactive. You wake up and respond to whatever comes. If someone discourages you, you stop. If someone praises you, you start. If a trend comes, you follow. If a problem comes, you panic. You spend life putting out fires instead of building a future.

A directionless person is not necessarily lazy. Many directionless people work hard. But their hard work is not organized. Their energy is not guided. Their time is not invested—it is spent.

Direction turns effort into progress.

HOW I LEARNED THE VALUE OF DIRECTION

There was a time in my life when I felt really lost, and it wasn't because I wasn't capable of doing things - it was because I didn't know which way to go. I would make decisions based on what others thought, how I felt at the moment, or what seemed like the easiest option. Living like that is really confusing, and confusion leads to putting things off. And when you put things off, you end up feeling sorry for what could have been.

As I slowly started to get back on my feet, I realized I had to figure out which way I was heading. I couldn't overhaul my entire life overnight, but I could pick one direction and stick to it. Making that decision had a ripple effect - it changed how I spent my time, the way I talked to people, how I made plans, and how I held myself accountable.

That is what direction does: it stops you from living randomly.

THE COMPASS METHOD: FOUR QUESTIONS THAT SHAPE DIRECTION

A strong direction can often be found by answering four simple questions honestly:

What problem do I want to solve?
Every meaningful direction solves a problem—either for you or for people. Education solves the problem of limited opportunities. Business solves the problem of value creation and income. Influence solves the problem of guidance and awareness. Choose a direction that solves something real.

What skill am I willing to master?
Direction without skill is like a dream without legs. Skill is what makes your direction practical. Ask yourself: what can I learn deeply? Writing, speaking, marketing, teaching, research, sales, leadership, technology, design—pick something you are willing to master.

What lifestyle am I willing to live?

Choosing a direction in life is a big decision, and it's not just about the end goal, but also about the journey. Every path you take has its own set of demands, like long hours, traveling, dealing with pressure, being in the public eye, or constantly needing to learn new things. If you pick a direction that comes with a lifestyle you can't handle, you'll likely give up on it. So, it's really important to select a direction that fits with a lifestyle you're okay with. This way, you can stick with it and make the most of your choices.

What impact do I want to leave?

Some individuals strive to leave a lasting legacy through their wealth, while others aim to be recalled for their selfless service to others. Then there are those who desire to be remembered for the positive change they've brought about. However, it's essential to note that making an impact doesn't necessarily have to be on a global scale - it can be within the confines of your own family, the community you're a part of, the students you teach, or the audience you cater to. The beauty of impact lies in its ability to give your life's direction a sense of purpose and meaning.

When you answer these questions, your direction becomes clearer.

Direction needs boundaries

Many people think direction means saying "yes" to a big dream. But direction also means saying "no" to distractions.

If you want direction, you must set boundaries:

boundaries with time-wasting habits,

boundaries with negative people,

boundaries with useless arguments,

boundaries with comfort that steals your future.

Without boundaries, direction becomes only words. With boundaries, direction becomes a lifestyle.

DIRECTION IS STRENGTHENED BY COMMITMENT, NOT BY MOOD

One of the biggest mistakes people make is they decide direction emotionally. They feel inspired one day and decide a huge plan. Then the inspiration fades and they stop. That is not direction. That is emotion.

Direction is not proven on the day you decide it. Direction is proven on the day you don't feel like it—and you still follow it.

If you want to determine direction, you must turn it into commitment:

commit to daily routine,

commit to learning,

commit to consistency,

commit to finishing what you start.

Direction becomes powerful when it becomes non-negotiable.

Two examples that show the power of direction

Let's take a look at someone like "Nelson Mandela", for instance. He had a clear sense of direction, even when things got really tough: he was all about freedom, justice, and dignity. What made his story so inspiring wasn't just that he was brave, but that he knew exactly what he wanted. When you're clear about what you stand for, it's harder for pressure to get to you. Having a sense of direction doesn't mean you won't feel pain - but it gives that pain a purpose, and it turns the things you give up into something that matters.

Let's take a look at someone like "The Imran Khan". No matter what people think of him, there's one thing we can all learn from his story: having a clear direction for a long time can have a big impact. When someone sticks to their goal for years, they start to gain credibility, trust, and a following. Having direction gives you the power to keep going even when others give up. It's what helps you stay focused and motivated, even when things get tough. And that's something we can all learn from, no matter what our goals are. By staying committed to one mission, you can build a movement and make a real difference.

These examples show that direction is not only about career. It is about clarity of purpose.

The greatest sign you have direction

How do you know your direction is real?

You begin to:

waste less time,

explain less to people,

focus more on skill,

say no to distractions,

accept sacrifice without complaining,

measure progress weekly, not daily,

keep moving even when results are slow.

Direction makes your life simpler. Not easier—but simpler. It reduces confusion.

FINAL LESSON

Figuring out which direction to go in life doesn't mean you have to have your entire future planned out. It just means you need to know what your next moves are going to be. It means you can stop drifting through life without a plan. You can stop letting other people's opinions and your emotions dictate what you do. It means you can stop trying a million different things and start focusing on building something that really matters.

And here is the final truth:

A person with direction may move slowly, but they will reach far.

A person without direction may move fast, but they will reach nowhere.

So, choose your direction carefully. Then protect it fiercely.

Because once your direction is clear, your life begins to rise—almost automatically—because your energy finally has a destination.

SELF-BUILDING
& DAILY ACTION

Self-Awareness

Self-awareness is the beginning of every real transformation.

You can change your city, your job, your friends, your clothes, even your lifestyle—and still remain the same person inside. But when you become self-aware, you begin to change from the root. You stop living on autopilot. You stop repeating patterns without understanding them. You stop being a stranger to your own mind.

Most people think success starts with motivation. I believe success starts with self-awareness. Because a person who does not understand himself will keep making the same mistakes with new excuses. He will blame people, blame time, blame luck, blame circumstances—but the truth will remain hidden: the real problem is inside, and the real solution is also inside.

Self-awareness is not self-criticism. It is self-truth.

It is the ability to look at yourself honestly and say:

"This is my strength."

"This is my weakness."

"This is what triggers me."

"This is what drains me."

"This is what makes me procrastinate."
"This is what makes me grow."
"This is the pattern I keep repeating."
"This is what I truly want."
"This is what I say I want, but my actions don't match."

Self-awareness is not comfort. It is clarity. And clarity is power.

THE DAY I REALIZED I WAS NOT "LAZY"—I WAS LOST

There was a time in my life when I used to think my biggest problem was laziness. I would start something and stop. I would plan and delay. I would feel excited for a day and then disappear for a week. People around me had their own explanations: "He is not serious," "He doesn't care," "He isn't made for study," "He isn't built for discipline."

I used to think those labels were true, that they defined me. I wore them like a badge, but a bad one. It took me a while to realize that I wasn't lazy, I was just "without direction". I didn't have a reason to get up and fight, to push through the tough times. I didn't have a clear idea of what I wanted, no vision to drive me forward. And without a plan that felt real, that felt like it was really going to happen, I just felt lost. When you don't know where you're going, it's hard to keep moving, because your mind can't see the point. You start to feel like you're just drifting, like you're not really living. But once I figured out that I wasn't lazy, that I was just lost, things started to change. I began to see that I had the power to create my own direction, to make my own plan, and to find my own meaning. And that's when everything started to fall into place.

That realization was one of the first self-awareness breakthroughs in my life: my problem was not intelligence. My problem was confusion. My problem was not "I can't." My problem was "I don't know how."

When you understand the real problem, you stop attacking yourself with shame—and you start building solutions with wisdom.

SELF-AWARENESS IS THE MIRROR YOU CANNOT AVOID

Most people avoid self-awareness because it is uncomfortable. It exposes your excuses. It reveals your patterns. It shows you the truth you hide from yourself.

But here is the reality: if you don't face yourself, life will force you to face yourself. Pain, failure, rejection, and disappointment become teachers when you ignore self-awareness.

Self-awareness is like a mirror. Some people avoid mirrors because they don't want to see flaws. But if you don't see your flaws, you can't fix them. And if you can't fix them, they will keep damaging your life quietly.

MY BIGGEST PATTERN: LISTENING TO EVERYONE EXCEPT MYSELF

When I look back at my early life, one pattern stands out clearly: I listened to too many people.

Someone might tell me that a particular field is pointless, and that would be enough to make me doubt my own thoughts and change my opinion.

Another would say, "You can't do it," and I would lose confidence. Someone would criticize me, and I would feel finished. Someone would praise me, and I would feel unstoppable. My emotions were controlled by voices. That is not maturity. That is confusion.

Self-awareness taught me that not every voice deserves access to my decisions. People can give opinions, but my life is my responsibility. And often, people speak from their fears, not from truth. When I became aware of this pattern, I started setting boundaries—not just boundaries with people, but boundaries with their influence on my mind.

Self-awareness made me stop living like a leaf in the wind.

SELF-AWARENESS AND SOCIAL MEDIA: WHY SOME CREATORS COLLAPSE

As my content journey grew, I learned that self-awareness becomes even more important when you have influence. Because when you start receiving attention, praise, criticism, and expectations, you can lose yourself easily.

Many creators become addicted to applause. They start chasing views more than value. They start changing their personality to match trends. They lose their authenticity. And inside, their peace disappears—even if their numbers increase.

Self-awareness protected me from that trap.
I had to ask myself constantly:
"Why am I creating?"
"Am I serving people or performing for people?"
"Am I building value or chasing validation?"

"Is my content aligned with my purpose or only with popularity?"

These questions kept me grounded. Because success without self-awareness can destroy you. The world may clap, but you will feel empty.

WHAT SELF-AWARENESS ACTUALLY GIVES YOU

Self-awareness gives you four major powers:

Power over your triggers

Everyone has triggers—words, situations, memories, comparisons, criticism. Triggers are dangerous because they push you into emotional decisions. Self-awareness helps you notice: "This thing makes me angry," "This makes me insecure," "This makes me give up." Once you notice, you can manage.

A person without self-awareness reacts.

A person with self-awareness responds.

Power over your patterns

Patterns are repeated behaviors. Some patterns build your life, some destroy it. Self-awareness helps you identify patterns like procrastination, overthinking, people-pleasing, fear of failure, laziness in routine, and addiction to comfort. Once you see the pattern, you can change the pattern.

Power over your energy

Not everything drains you equally. Some people drain you. Some habits drain you. Some environments drain you. Self-awareness helps you protect your energy by making better choices.

Power over your identity

Many people don't know who they are. They define themselves by failures, by people's opinions, by childhood experiences, by society labels. Self-awareness helps you define yourself by your values and your direction.

HOW I BUILT SELF-AWARENESS IN REAL LIFE

Self-awareness didn't arrive to me as a sudden miracle. I built it through painful honesty and daily reflection.

I started asking myself difficult questions after failure. Not "Who is to blame?" but "What can I learn?" I began noticing what I did when life was hard. Did I run? Did I blame? Did I delay? Did I escape? That observation became a teacher.

I also learned to observe my mind like an outsider. When I felt negative thoughts, I asked: "Is this thought true? Or is it fear?" When I felt laziness, I asked: "Am I tired or am I avoiding discomfort?" When I felt pressure, I asked: "Am I overthinking outcomes instead of focusing on actions?"

These questions may look small, but they are life-changing. Because your life improves when your awareness improves.

THE DANGEROUS ILLUSION: THINKING YOU KNOW YOURSELF

Many people say, "I know myself." But their habits prove they don't.

If you truly know yourself, you will know:

what motivates you,

what distracts you,

what breaks your confidence,
what strengthens you,
what environment makes you grow,
what people make you weak,
what goals truly matter to you.

Self-awareness is not a claim. It is a practice.

And the deeper you go, the more you realize: we all have blind spots. Even strong people have blind spots. That is why self-awareness is a lifelong process, not a one-time lesson.

A SIMPLE SELF-AWARENESS EXERCISE

If you want practical self-awareness, start with this:

Every night, ask yourself three questions:

1. What did you accomplish today that helped you make progress and feel like you're getting closer to your goals?
2. What did I do today that held me back?
3. What is one thing I will improve tomorrow?

If you're truthful with yourself for just a month, you'll be amazed at the difference it can make. See, when you have a good understanding of yourself, you start to make changes. And those changes lead to real progress.

THE FINAL LESSON

Self-awareness is not about being perfect. It is about being conscious. It is about seeing your life clearly enough that you can guide it wisely.

When you become self-aware, you stop being surprised by your own mistakes. You stop repeating the same pattern. You stop living by emotion. You stop acting like a victim. You start becoming a leader of your own life.

And that is the deepest truth:

The person who understands himself will always have an advantage over the person who doesn't—because self-awareness is the foundation of every comeback.

Self-Accountability

Self-accountability is the moment you stop being a commentator on your life and start being the owner of your life.

Most people can explain why their life is not working. They can describe their problems with perfect detail. They can list the reasons: family issues, financial pressure, bad luck, toxic people, unfair systems, wrong timing, lack of support. Some of these reasons are real—life is not equally easy for everyone. But there is one truth that separates people who rise from people who remain stuck:

A person who rises takes responsibility even when the circumstances are unfair.

Self-accountability does not mean you blame yourself for everything. It means you stop using excuses as a lifestyle. It means you understand this powerful principle: even if something is not your fault, it is still your responsibility to fix it.

Taking control of your life is liberating. When you own up to your actions, you're actually setting yourself free. The moment you stop blaming others and start taking responsibility, you gain the power to make changes. If you always think that your life is the way it is because of something someone else did, you'll feel helpless. But when you realize that your life is what it is because of the choices you've made, that's when you become powerful. And the best part is, choices can be changed, so you have the freedom to create the life you want.

THE SILENT ENEMY: THE EXCUSE THAT SOUNDS LOGICAL

Excuses rarely sound stupid. If excuses sounded foolish, nobody would believe them. Excuses usually sound logical, reasonable, and even intelligent. That is why they are dangerous.

"I'm tired."

"I'm busy."

"I have stress."

"I don't have support."

"I'm not in the mood."

"People don't give me opportunities."

"I will start when conditions improve."

All these statements can be true sometimes. But self-accountability asks a deeper question:

Even if this is true, what can I do today?

Because accountable people don't wait for the perfect life. They build progress inside imperfect life.

THE DAY I STOPPED DEFENDING MY FAILURE

I used to make excuses for my weaknesses. If I was late, I had a reason. If I gave up, I had an excuse. If I failed, I blamed someone or something else. I'd blame the situation, or the pressure, or the negative people around me, or not having enough resources. But really, I was just trying to protect myself from looking bad. I didn't want to admit that I wasn't good enough, so I made up stories to explain why things didn't go my way. It was easier to blame something outside of myself than to take responsibility for my own failures.

But one day I realized a painful truth: my excuses were not protecting me—they were keeping me small.

The world doesn't reward explanation. The world rewards results.

This was one of the biggest turning points in my growth: I stopped defending my failure and started correcting my habits. I stopped asking, "Why is this happening to me?" and started asking, "What am I doing that is keeping me here?"

That shift is self-accountability.

ACCOUNTABILITY IS A MIRROR, NOT A MICROPHONE

Many people use their mouth too much and their mind too little. They talk about problems instead of solving them. They complain about the system but never build their skill. They criticize others but never improve themselves. They discuss life instead of changing life.

Self-accountability is the opposite. It is quiet. It is personal. It is private.

Accountability is not you announcing your goals to everyone. Accountability is you facing yourself when nobody is watching. It is you asking: "Did I do what I said I would do?" "Did I keep my promise to myself?" "Did I waste today?" "Did I move forward?"

A person who takes responsibility for their actions doesn't need to broadcast it to the world; they just need to be honest with themselves.

WHAT SELF-ACCOUNTABILITY ACTUALLY MEANS

Self-accountability means you accept four realities:

Reality 1: Your life is a result of your repeated choices.
Not one choice. Repeated choices. Your habits are voting for your future daily.

Reality 2: Nobody is coming to rescue you.
Support can help, but it cannot replace your effort. Mentors can guide, but they cannot do the work. Friends can motivate, but they cannot build your discipline. At the end, your life is your responsibility.

Reality 3: Feelings are not reliable leaders.
If you wait to "feel ready," you will remain stuck. Accountable people work even when they don't feel like it, because they understand that emotions are temporary but discipline is permanent.

Reality 4: The pain of discipline is cheaper than the pain of regret.
Regret is heavy. Discipline is hard, but regret is harder.

MY SOCIAL MEDIA LESSON: ACCOUNTABILITY WHEN NO ONE CLAPS

When I began creating content, the easy option was to stop. Silence is discouraging. Low views make you question everything. And for a long time, the results did not match the effort. That is where accountability becomes real.

Because in that stage, nobody can force you. Nobody can monitor you. Nobody will punish you if you stop.

Only your future will punish you.

So, I had to hold myself accountable. I had to decide: "Even if nobody is watching, I will keep improving. Even if today's post gets no response, I will still show up tomorrow." That is accountability: continuing without applause.

This applies to many areas of life, like education, writing, and business. At first, the work you put in isn't always noticeable. But it's during these behind-the-scenes times that you need to stay on track and be responsible, because the progress you make then is what leads to the successes that people can see later on. You have to be willing to put in the effort when it doesn't seem like it's making a difference, because that's what will ultimately get you to where you want to be.

THE THREE TYPES OF ACCOUNTABILITIES

There are three levels of self-accountability, and all three are needed.

Accountability of time

Time accountability means you respect your hours. You stop spending time like it is unlimited. You plan your day. You protect your prime hours. You reduce distractions. You stop giving your best hours to useless things and your leftovers to your dreams.

A person who respects time respects life.

Accountability of standards

Standards are the rules you live by. For example: "I will not lie," "I will not cheat," "I will not quit," "I will not waste my mornings," "I will not stay in toxic circles," "I will not be lazy with my goals."

Without standards, life becomes random. With standards, life becomes structured.

Accountability of results

Results accountability means you track progress. Not perfection—progress. You measure. You review. You adjust. You don't just "feel busy." You prove movement.

Accountable people don't only work. They check: "Is my work producing something?"

THE HARDEST PART: ACCOUNTABILITY WITHOUT SELF-HATE

Many people avoid accountability because they confuse it with self-hate. They think being accountable means being harsh, being cruel, being negative to themselves. That is wrong.

Self-accountability is not self-hate. It is self-leadership.

A leader doesn't insult his team daily. A leader guides, corrects, and improves. You must treat yourself like your own leader. Be honest, but also be wise. Be strict with habits, but gentle with growth. Correct yourself without breaking yourself.

If you fail one day, don't use it as proof that you are weak. Use it as feedback. Learn. Adjust. Continue.

PRACTICAL ACCOUNTABILITY: HOW TO BECOME ACCOUNTABLE DAILY

Here are simple practices that build strong self-accountability:

Write your day before you live it. Even a simple plan reduces confusion.

Choose 3 non-negotiable tasks daily. If you complete them, you win the day.

Track one habit for 30 days. Tracking creates awareness. Awareness creates correction.

Ask yourself every night: "Did I respect my time today?"

Stop blaming and start building: when something goes wrong, ask "What can I control?"

Keep promises small but consistent: big promises break, small promises build identity.

TWO EXAMPLES THAT SHOW ACCOUNTABILITY

Let's take "Cathy Freeman" as a great example. People often remember her historic win, but what's really important is the hard work she put in behind the scenes. She showed up to training every day, even when no one was watching, and she didn't make excuses when things got tough. She stayed disciplined and kept going, even when everyone's expectations were high. Her story teaches us that success isn't just about being talented - it's about being accountable and holding yourself to a high standard every single day, especially when things get difficult.

Let's take a look at "Ash Barty" as a great example. Her career is a perfect illustration of what it means to be accountable in a calm and mature way. She knows exactly when to put in the work, when to take a step back and reset, and how to keep her mental strength even when things get tough. It's not just about being motivated all the time - she's all about sticking to a routine, practicing consistently, and being in control of her emotions. What we can learn from her is that being accountable isn't just about pushing yourself nonstop, it's also about making smart choices, staying true to your values, and protecting your focus so you can perform at your best over time. By doing so, you can achieve a sense of balance and stability that will help you succeed in the long run.

THE FINAL LESSON

Self-accountability is the bridge between your potential and your reality. Potential is cheap. Everyone has potential. But accountable people turn potential into results.

If you want to rise again, you must become accountable—not to people, but to yourself.

Because at the end, nobody will live your life for you. Nobody will carry your regret. Nobody will pay the cost of your delay. That cost belongs to you.

You should take responsibility for your actions, not because things are always simple, but because what's ahead of you really matters.

And remember this truth:
When you take responsibility, you take power. And when you take power, you take control of your destiny.

Unnecessary Burden

There is a kind of tiredness that sleep cannot fix.

It is not the tiredness of work. It is not the tiredness of long hours. It is the tiredness of carrying weight that was never meant to be yours—weight you picked up slowly, quietly, without noticing, until one day you looked at your life and wondered: Why do I feel so heavy even when I'm trying so hard?

That heaviness is often not your circumstances. It is your unnecessary burden.

An unnecessary burden is anything you carry in your mind, heart, or identity that does not serve your growth. It doesn't solve a problem, it doesn't improve your character, it doesn't move you forward—yet it drains your energy every day. It can be a thought you keep repeating. It can be shame you keep feeding. It can be an old label you never removed. It can be a fear you accepted as truth. It can be a standard you copied from people who don't live your life.

The saddest part is this: most people don't know they are carrying unnecessary burdens. They think this is normal. They think this is "life." They think this is their personality. They think this is reality. But it isn't. It is just weight.

And weight changes everything.

When you carry weight, your speed decreases. Your focus breaks. Your confidence weakens. You become easily irritated. You overthink small things. You delay big things. You start avoiding challenges not because you are incapable—but because you are already exhausted from carrying what you should have dropped long ago.

I learned this truth the hard way.

There was a season in my life when I was not recognized, not celebrated, not followed by crowds, not holding any title that impressed people. I was living quietly in a flat in Aziz Bhatti Town, Sargodha—trying to rebuild myself in a world that didn't notice me. From the outside it looked like "normal struggle." But inside, I was carrying invisible weight: the fear of being judged, the pain of being underestimated, the pressure to prove something, the shame of past failure, the anxiety of "what if I never become anything?"

No one could see that burden. But I felt it in my chest. I felt it in my thoughts. I felt it in my sleep. I felt it in the way I looked at my own future.

And that is why I say: the heaviest burdens are not carried in the hands. They are carried in the head.

The burden of old labels

One of the first unnecessary burdens people carry is an old label.

You failed once, and you start calling yourself a failure.

You made a mistake, and you start calling yourself weak.

You were rejected, and you start calling yourself not good enough.

You struggled, and you start calling yourself unlucky.

Labels become cages when you stop treating them as "something that happened" and start treating them as "who I am."

When I failed in school, the pain was real. But what was heavier than the result was the story that followed it—what people said, what they expected now, the way they looked at me, the way I started looking at myself. If you are not careful, one moment becomes your identity. And when your identity becomes small, your actions become small too.

The moment your life changes is the moment you say: That happened, but that is not me.

You don't need to deny the past. You need to stop living inside it.

The burden of proving yourself to everyone

Another unnecessary burden is the hunger to prove your worth to people.

It sounds strong, but it is actually a trap. Because it never ends.

If you succeed, some people will say you got lucky.

If you achieve something, some people will say it's not enough.

If you rise, some people will look for a reason to pull you down.

If your heart is addicted to external approval, your peace will always be in someone else's hands. You will work, but you will not feel satisfied. You will grow, but you will not feel complete. Because your success will always be measured by an audience that changes its mind every day.

I felt this burden in my early journey—especially when I was still unheard. When you are struggling, you naturally want respect. You want someone to say, "I believe in you." You want someone to clap. But clapping does not build a life. Discipline builds a life.

Real freedom begins when you stop trying to impress people who are not building anything themselves.

The burden of borrowed expectations

Sometimes the burden is not shame or fear. Sometimes the burden is expectations—borrowed from family, society, culture, or friends.

People tell you what success should look like.

They tell you what career is "respectable."

They tell you when you should achieve.

They tell you how you should live.

They tell you what is "right" for you without understanding your nature.

You try to follow their map, but the map was never made for your journey.

And the moment you live by someone else's expectations, you start losing yourself. You become busy, but not fulfilled. You become productive, but not peaceful. You might even "win" something, but inside you feel empty—because it wasn't your dream. It was theirs.

This is why determining your own direction matters. Not because you reject people—but because you respect your own soul enough to choose your path.

The burden of perfectionism

Perfectionism is a polite form of fear.

It says, "Wait."

It says, "Not yet."

It says, "Make it flawless first."

It says, "If it's not perfect, don't show it."

But life rewards progress, not perfection.

Perfectionism makes people delay their dreams until the dream dies quietly. They keep editing, fixing, planning, preparing—until years pass and the only thing they perfected is procrastination.

I remember content creation days when I could have waited for "perfect lighting," "perfect editing," "perfect setup," "perfect confidence." If I had waited for perfection, I would still be waiting. Instead, I learned something more valuable: start with what you have, improve on the way.

The real secret is not being perfect. The real secret is being consistent.

The burden of overthinking

Overthinking is a burden that pretends to be intelligence.

A person thinks they are being "careful," but they are actually being trapped. The mind keeps running, calculating, replaying, predicting, imagining failure, imagining embarrassment, imagining loss—until action becomes impossible.

Overthinking is not planning. Planning produces a step. Overthinking produces a loop.

One simple way to recognize overthinking is this: if your thinking is not producing action, it is producing anxiety.

Some people carry this burden for years. They don't fail because they lack ability. They fail because they never begin. They keep living in the mind instead of living in the mission.

When I was trying to rebuild my future, there were nights when my mind created a thousand negative movies: "What if I try and fail again?" "What if people laugh?" "What if nothing changes?" That is when I learned to respond to my own mind like a leader: We will think, but we will not drown. We will plan, then we will move.

Your mind is a powerful tool—but if you don't control it, it becomes a prison.

The burden of resentment

Resentment is carrying someone's mistake inside your heart.

It feels justified. It feels logical. It feels like you are protecting your dignity. But resentment doesn't punish the other person—it punishes you. It keeps your mind trapped in old scenes. It keeps your emotions tied to someone else's behavior. It steals your energy from the present and donates it to the past.

I have learned that you don't need to keep pain to prove you were wronged. You can release pain and still remember the lesson. You can move forward and still protect your boundaries.

Forgiveness is not saying, "It was okay."

Forgiveness is saying, "I am not paying for it anymore."

That is why forgiveness is not weakness. It is strength with wisdom.

The burden of carrying tomorrow's problems today

Many people suffer twice.

They suffer for what is happening today.

And they suffer for what might happen tomorrow.

They carry future pain like it is already real. They carry imagined failures like they already happened. They carry fears like they are facts.

This is one of the biggest unnecessary burdens: living in a future that has not arrived.

Worry does not prepare you. It drains you.

Preparation is different. Preparation is action: learning, planning, saving, practicing, improving. Worry is just emotional noise.

One of the most powerful habits I ever learned was simple: do what you can today, and leave the rest for tomorrow. Life is built in days, not in anxiety.

The burden of silence after effort

There is also a burden that creators and builders understand deeply: the burden of giving effort and receiving silence.

You post, and nothing happens.

You speak, and no one responds.

You work, and nobody recognizes.

You try, and results delay.

Silence can become an unnecessary burden if you start interpreting it as rejection. If you start taking it personally. If you start thinking silence means you are not valuable.

I lived through that silence. I remember uploading again and again and seeing low response. I remember moments when I felt like I was talking to an empty world. But then I learned: silence is not always a sign to stop. Sometimes silence is a season that trains your endurance.

And endurance is expensive. It costs ego. It costs comfort. It costs patience.

But it also produces something priceless: inner strength.

The burden of carrying success like a fear

This may sound strange, but it is real: some people carry fear even when they start rising.

They fear losing progress.

They fear not meeting expectations.

They fear people's jealousy.

They fear responsibility.

So instead of enjoying growth, they live in tension. They turn success into another burden.

The solution is to remember: you don't need to carry success with fear. You need to carry it with discipline and humility. Do your work. Improve your character. Stay grounded. Let results come—and let them go if needed. Because your identity should not be your numbers. Your identity should be your principles.

How to drop unnecessary burdens

Dropping unnecessary burdens is not one dramatic moment. It is a practice.

First, you must ask one honest question: What am I carrying that is not helping me build my future?

Name it. Be specific. Not "stress." What kind of stress? Is it comparison? Is it regret? Is it approval addiction? Is it resentment? Is it perfectionism? Is it fear of judgment?

Second, ask another question: Is this burden mine—or did I borrow it?

Some burdens are borrowed from people.

Some burdens are borrowed from society.

Some burdens are borrowed from childhood.

Some burdens are borrowed from past mistakes.

If it is borrowed, return it.

Third, replace emotional weight with daily structure. Burdens grow in empty space. When your day has no routine, the mind starts carrying unnecessary stories. But when your day has purpose—study time, work time, health time, creation time—your mind becomes calmer because it has direction.

Fourth, make peace with being misunderstood. This is a big one. Many burdens come from trying to explain yourself to everyone. But not everyone will understand you. And that's okay. Your job is not to win everyone's approval. Your job is to win your future.

The final lesson

Life will give you real burdens: responsibility, challenges, pressure, setbacks, losses. Those burdens are part of becoming strong.

But unnecessary burdens are optional.

You don't need to carry old labels.

You don't need to carry everyone's opinions.

You don't need to carry resentment.

You don't need to carry perfectionism.

You don't need to carry tomorrow's fear today.

You don't need to carry guilt that never becomes growth.

Drop what is not building you.

Because the truth is simple: when you remove unnecessary weight, you don't just feel lighter—you move faster. You think clearer. You breathe deeper. You work better. You rise stronger.

And when you rise, you'll realize something that changes everything:

It was never your destiny that was heavy.

It was the burden you kept carrying for too long.

Not From Tomorrow, But From Today

Tomorrow is the most dangerous word in the world.

Not because tomorrow is bad—tomorrow is beautiful. But because "tomorrow" is the favorite hiding place of fear, laziness, and self-doubt. Tomorrow is where people place their unfinished dreams, their delayed decisions, their ignored responsibilities, and their unfulfilled potential. Tomorrow is where good intentions go to sleep.

I have seen it again and again—people who are talented, intelligent, and full of ideas, yet their lives remain stuck for one simple reason: they keep postponing their beginning.

They say, "I will start tomorrow."

They say it like a promise. But most of the time, it is not a promise. It is an escape.

Because starting tomorrow feels safe. Starting tomorrow feels comfortable. Starting tomorrow allows you to remain the same today. And that is exactly why many people love tomorrow—it gives them permission to stay in their comfort zone.

But a life changes only when a person begins.
Not from tomorrow.
From today.

WHY PEOPLE CHOOSE "TOMORROW"

Let's be honest: people don't delay because they don't want success.
They delay because they are afraid of the process.

There are many reasons people say "tomorrow":

1) Fear of failure.
If you start today, you might fail today. If you delay, you can still live
in the illusion that you "could" succeed. Tomorrow protects your ego.
Today tests your courage.

2) Fear of judgment.
When you start, you become visible. People may criticize. People
may laugh. People may doubt. So you delay to avoid the pain of being
seen while you are still learning.

3) Fear of discomfort.
Change is uncomfortable. Discipline is uncomfortable. Effort is
uncomfortable. The mind prefers comfort, so it negotiates: "Not
now. Later."

4) Perfectionism.
People tell themselves, "I will start when I have more resources,
more time, better tools, better confidence, better mood." They wait
for perfection—and perfection never arrives.

5) Lack of clarity.

Some people delay because they don't know where to begin. They feel overwhelmed, so they do nothing. But clarity often comes "after" you start, not before.

6) The addiction to quick results.

If they can't see instant progress, they lose interest. They start something for two days, don't see results, and then go back to tomorrow.

All these reasons have one thing in common: they keep people in the same place.

THE RISK OF TOMORROW

The biggest risk of tomorrow is not failure. The biggest risk of tomorrow is "regret".

Because delay doesn't look dangerous in one day. It looks harmless. But when delay becomes a habit, it steals your years.

Tomorrow becomes a lifestyle.

Then months pass.

Then years pass.

Then you wake up and say, "Where did my life go?"

A person who keeps delaying doesn't always lose because of lack of talent. They lose because time ran out while they were preparing to begin.

The tragedy is this: many people don't fail in life. They simply never start.

THE DAY I UNDERSTOOD THE POWER OF TODAY

There was a phase of my life when "tomorrow" was my comfort too. I used to delay because I wasn't confident. I used to delay because I didn't feel ready. I used to delay because I listened to people's voices more than my own potential.

But when life hit me with failure, I realized something: tomorrow is not guaranteed, but today is in your hands.

When I failed in school, it didn't just hurt my result—it shook my identity. It was easy to hide. It was easy to disappear. It was easy to accept the label people were giving me. And for a moment, that darkness felt like my reality. My mind kept telling me, "It's finished. You can't rise. You are not made for study. You have no direction."

If I had accepted that voice, my whole story would have ended there.

But something changed inside me: I got tired of suffering without growth. I got tired of feeling ashamed without fighting back. I got tired of watching life move forward while I stayed stuck.

And I realized: if my life is going to change, it will not change through wishing.

It will change through starting.

So, I started again. Not perfectly. Not with full confidence. Not with perfect resources. But I started.

That decision was not made in a perfect environment. It was made in pressure, in fear, in uncertainty. And that is the point: the best beginnings are not perfect—they are courageous.

STARTING TODAY WITH LESS RESOURCES

Many people think they must have everything to begin. But life doesn't give you everything first. Life gives you a chance—and then you build.

If you wait for the perfect time, you will wait forever.

When I started rebuilding myself, I didn't have a smooth road. I didn't have people cheering daily. I didn't have everything organized. I didn't have a powerful platform from day one. I didn't have millions of followers. I didn't even have confidence all the time.

But I had one thing: willingness to begin with what I had.

That is the real secret: success is not built by those who have the most resources. Success is built by those who use what they have, where they are, and begin anyway.

Some people have money but no discipline.

Some people have support but no seriousness.

Some people have talent but no consistency.

And some people have very little—but they start, and that start becomes a miracle over time.

THE POWER OF SMALL STARTS

Starting today doesn't mean doing everything today. It means doing something today.

Start small. But start real.

Read one page.

Write one paragraph.

Record one short video.

Walk ten minutes.

Study one topic.

Send one proposal.

Make one phone call.

Fix one habit.

Small starts are powerful because they break the greatest enemy: inertia.

Inertia is the force that keeps you stuck. Once you break it, progress becomes easier.

That is why the first step is always the hardest step. Because you are not only moving your body—you are moving your mindset.

WHY I DIDN'T WAIT FOR PERMISSION

When I started creating content, nobody gave me permission. Nobody said, "Yes, you are ready." Nobody officially declared, "Now you are an influencer." The early days were silent. Uploading content and seeing little response can make you feel invisible. And in that invisibility, tomorrow becomes tempting: "Maybe I'll try later. Maybe it's not for me."

But I learned: the world doesn't give you permission to be great. You give yourself permission through action.

So, I kept going.

I recorded. I edited. I uploaded. I improved. And I repeated.

Even if the resources were limited, the commitment was strong.

Even if the results were slow, the process was real.

And slowly, today started building tomorrow.

That is the formula: when you respect today, tomorrow respects you.

THE PSYCHOLOGY OF TODAY

There is a powerful psychological truth: your brain begins to believe what your actions repeat.

If you delay daily, your brain learns: "We don't finish."

If you start daily, your brain learns: "We are serious."

If you quit daily, your brain learns: "We are weak."

If you continue daily, your brain learns: "We are strong."

So, starting today is not only about progress—it is about identity.

Every time you start today, you become the type of person who starts.

Every time you delay, you become the type of person who delays.

This is why "today" is not a date. Today is a character decision.

WHAT HAPPENS IF YOU KEEP SAYING TOMORROW

Let me be direct: if you keep saying tomorrow, three things will happen.

First, your confidence will decrease. Because confidence is built by action, not by thinking.

Second, your fear will increase. Because fear grows in delay.

Third, your regrets will multiply. Because time will pass whether you move or not.

Tomorrow is not harmless. Tomorrow is expensive.

A MESSAGE FOR THE READER

If you are reading this while feeling behind, I want to tell you something clearly:

You don't need more time.

You need more courage.

You don't need perfect conditions.

You need a decision.

You don't need the best resources.

You need the best consistency.

Start from where you are. Use what you have. Do what you can. Begin today.

Because the world changes only after you change. And you change the moment you stop negotiating with your future.

FINAL LESSON

Not from tomorrow, but from today—this is not a motivational quote. It is a life strategy.

Today is where habits are built.

Today is where discipline is trained.

Today is where skills are developed.

Today is where dreams become real.

And if you take one step today, you have already defeated the biggest enemy: delay.

So don't ask, "Will I succeed?"

Ask, "Will I start?"

Because the person who starts today has already done what most people never do.

They began.

And that beginning is the first proof that they are ready to rise again.

Goal to Action

Most people don't fail because they don't have goals. They fail because their goals remain trapped in their head.

They say, "I want to be successful."

They say, "I want to study again."

They say, "I want to write a book."

They say, "I want to start a business."

They say, "I want to change my life."

But wanting is not a system. Wanting is emotion. Wanting is a beautiful feeling—but it is not a plan. And a goal without a plan becomes a wish. It stays attractive in the mind but invisible in reality.

Here's the thing: setting a goal is one thing, but making it happen is another story. The key is to break it down into smaller, manageable tasks that you can tackle every day. When you do this, something cool happens - your brain doesn't feel so overwhelmed, you can actually see how far you've come, and you start to feel motivated because you're making progress. It's like taking a big puzzle and turning it into smaller, easier-to-solve pieces. By doing so, you make your goal feel more real, more achievable, and that's when the magic happens.

That is why this chapter is not about dreaming bigger. It is about executing smarter.

***

WHY PEOPLE SAY "TOMORROW" (AND WHAT IT COSTS)

Before we talk about goals, we must talk about "tomorrow," because "tomorrow" is where goals go to sleep—and sometimes never wake up.

People delay for many reasons, but most of those reasons are psychological:

1) Fear of failure

If you start today, you might fail today. If you delay, you can still live in the illusion that you "could" succeed. Tomorrow protects the ego. Today tests the courage.

2) Fear of judgment

Starting makes you visible. People may laugh, criticize, doubt, or compare. Many people delay not because they can't do it, but because they can't tolerate being seen while learning.

3) Comfort addiction

Change is uncomfortable. Discipline is uncomfortable. New routines are uncomfortable. So the mind negotiates: "Not now, later."

4) Perfectionism

"I will start when I have better tools, more time, more money, more confidence, a better mood." Perfectionism is fear in a clean dress. It feels responsible, but it is actually delay.

5) Overwhelm

Some people don't start because they don't know where to begin. Their goal feels huge, so they freeze. They think, "If I can't do everything, I will do nothing."

6) Love for quick results

If results don't come fast, they lose interest. They start for two days, don't see change, and return to tomorrow.

The risk of "tomorrow" is not that you delay one day. The risk is you develop a habit of delay. And the habit of delay quietly steals years.

The sad truth is that a lot of people don't actually fail at what they want to do. The real problem is that they never even try to start.

***

THE DAY I REALIZED SMALL TASKS CHANGE BIG DESTINY

There were seasons in my life where big goals felt impossible. You look at the distance and your mind panics. You look at your resources and you feel ashamed. You look at your past and you feel uncertain. In those moments, "tomorrow" feels like comfort. It feels like a safe place where you can keep dreaming without risking anything.

I realized that the truth is simple: it's what you do today that really matters, not what you plan to do tomorrow.

Going back to school was a big deal for me. My goal was huge - getting a doctorate degree. It's a pretty inspiring idea, but it's also overwhelming. If you focus too much on the end result, it can feel exhausting even before you start working towards it. I mean, thinking about reaching the top of the mountain can be daunting, and it's easy to feel tired just thinking about it. But I knew I had to break it down into smaller steps and take it one step at a time. That way, the journey wouldn't feel so impossible.

So I learned to break it down. I stopped carrying the whole mountain in my head. I started carrying only today's step: today's reading, today's writing, today's revision, today's submission, today's progress.

The same principle applied when I started content creation. " Become an influencer" is not a daily action. But "record one video today" is a daily action. " Write one script today" is a daily action. " Upload one piece of content today" is a daily action.

That is how goals become real: through tasks.

Big results are not built by big emotions.

Big results are built by small steps repeated.

***

THE DIFFERENCE BETWEEN A DREAM, A GOAL, AND A TASK

Let's make it clear:

A dream is what you want.

A goal is what you decide.

A task is what you do.

Dream: "I want a new life."

Goal: "I will complete my education and build my career."

Task: "Today I will study 60 minutes, write 300 words, and revise notes."

Dream: "I want to write a book."

Goal: "I will finish a full draft in 90 days."

Task: "Today I will write 900 words."

If you stay at dream level, your life stays emotional.

If you move to goal level, your life becomes serious.

If you move to task level, your life becomes unstoppable.

Because tasks are the language of results.

***

STEP 1: SET GOALS THE RIGHT WAY (THE 4S METHOD)

Most people set goals that sound good but don't guide action. They write goals like slogans—beautiful sentences with no structure.

Here is a simple method that works:

1) Specific

Bad: "I want success."

Good: "I want to write and publish my book."

Bad: "I want to study."

Good: "I will study two hours daily."

2) Simple

If a goal is too complex, it becomes confusing. Confusion kills consistency.

Your goal should be simple, something you can sum up in just one sentence, so it's clear and easy to understand what you're trying to achieve.

3) Scheduled

A goal without a time frame becomes a wish.

Time creates urgency.

Instead of: "Someday I will…"
Write: "In 12 weeks I will…"

4) Supported by routine

This is the most important. A goal must have a routine attached to it.

A strong goal is written like this:
"I will achieve X by Y date by doing Z routine."

Example:
"I will complete my book draft in 60 days by writing 800 words daily."
"I will improve my fitness in 12 weeks by walking 30 minutes daily."
"I will build my platform by posting one video daily for 100 days."

When your goal includes routine, it becomes executable.

***

STEP 2: BREAK YOUR GOAL INTO TASKS (THE LADDER SYSTEM)

A goal is the top floor. Tasks are the stairs.

If you try to jump to the top, you fall.

If you climb step by step, you rise.

Here is the Ladder System:

Level 1: Outcome goal (big result)

Example: "Finish my book."

Level 2: Monthly target

Example: "Write 4 chapters this month."

Level 3: Weekly target

Example: "Write 1 chapter this week."

Level 4: Daily tasks

Example: "Write 800–1,000 words today."

Your mind feels at ease now, it's clear about what needs to be done.

Most people stay at Level 1 only. They keep repeating the big goal and feel motivated for one day, then overwhelmed for ten days. The ladder system turns motivation into structure.

STEP 3: MAKE TASKS SMALL ENOUGH THAT YOU CANNOT REFUSE

The best plan is not the biggest plan. The best plan is the plan you will follow even on a bad day.

If you write: "Study 6 hours daily," you may quit in three days.

If you just write down "study 45 minutes every day", you might actually stick to it for months.

Small tasks are not weak. They are strategic.

Small tasks build momentum, and momentum is stronger than motivation.

On days when you feel low, reduce the task, don't cancel it.

If you can't write 1,000 words, write 200.

If you can't walk 30 minutes, walk 10.

Don't worry if you can't make a whole video, just record a quick message instead.

The rule is: never break the chain.

STEP 4: USE THE "TOP 3" RULE DAILY

To make progress towards your goal, pick three important tasks each day that will help you get closer to achieving it.

Not 20 tasks. Not 10 tasks. Only 3.

Because too many tasks scatter you.

Three tasks focus you.

Example for writer:

1. Write 900 words

2. Edit yesterday's section

3. Outline next section

Example for student:

1. Read 10 pages

2. Write notes

3. Practice questions

Example for content creator:

1. Record a video
2. Edit and upload
3. Engage with audience 15 minutes

When you complete your Top 3, you win the day.
A winning day repeated becomes a winning year.

***

STEP 5: TRACK YOUR PROGRESS (WITHOUT EMOTION, WITH HONESTY)

A goal without tracking is a goal without truth.
Tracking doesn't mean stress. Tracking means awareness.
If you don't measure, you can't improve.
Write down:
What you did today
What you didn't do
Why you didn't do it
What you will improve tomorrow
When you track, you become accountable.
When you become accountable, your growth becomes faster.

STEP 6: BUILD A "TOMORROW DEFENSE" PLAN (RELAPSE PLAN)

Even strong people fall into tomorrow thinking. The issue is not falling. The issue is staying down.
So, create a rule for yourself:

When your mind says "tomorrow," respond:
"Do the smallest version today."
This defeats delay without pressure.
Because action breaks fear.
And fear is the fuel of tomorrow.

STEP 7: CREATE A REWARD SYSTEM (MAKE PROGRESS ENJOYABLE)

Your mind repeats what it is rewarded for.
So, reward progress.
After completing tasks, take a short break
Celebrate milestones (chapter completed, week completed)
Give yourself positive feedback
Share progress with someone supportive
This is not childish. It is psychology.
When progress feels meaningful, consistency becomes easier.

STEP 8: THE "START WITH WHAT YOU HAVE" PRINCIPLE

Many people delay because they think they lack resources.
But life doesn't give you everything first. Life gives you a chance first.
Start with:
the phone you have
the time you have
the knowledge you have
the place you are in
the energy you have
Starting with less resources builds the strongest skill: resourcefulness.

Putting things off until everything is just right only teaches you one thing: how to wait.

STEP 9: WEEKLY REVIEW (THE COURSE CORRECTION)

One mistake people make is they judge themselves daily.

Some days are productive, some are not.

The real evaluation should be weekly.

Every week ask:

What worked?

What didn't work?

What distracted me?

What is the next improvement?

A weekly review turns you into a strategist, not an emotional worker.

STEP 10: YOUR GOAL SHOULD SHAPE YOUR IDENTITY

The real power of having goals isn't just about achieving them, it's about who you become in the process.

When you do daily tasks, you become a disciplined person.

When you keep promises, you become reliable to yourself.

When you stay consistent, you become strong.

This identity becomes your real success.

Because even if a goal changes, a strong identity keeps winning.

FINAL MESSAGE

Don't wait around for the perfect moment to take action - it's just not going to happen. The truth is, the only time that really matters is the present. So, instead of putting things off until everything feels just right, why not start making progress now? It's the only way to make your goals and dreams a reality.

Set goals that are clear.

Break them into tasks that are small.

Do the tasks daily.

Track progress weekly.

And when your mind says "tomorrow," do one small thing today.

Because the biggest difference between dreamers and achievers is simple:

Dreamers plan.

Achievers execute.

And execution begins with one small task—done today.

The Momentum Rule

Motivation is beautiful—but it is not reliable.

When your drive to succeed is based on how you feel, your progress is going to be all over the place. There will be days when you're on top of the world, and days when you feel completely drained. Some days you'll be super productive, and others you'll barely get anything done - it's like your dreams and goals don't even matter. This is why a lot of people start out strong, but then fizzle out. It's not that they're not capable of achieving their goals, it's just that they're relying too much on their emotions to get them through.

The truth is: success is not built by the person who feels motivated every day. Success is built by the person who knows how to move even when motivation is low.

And this is where momentum becomes the real secret.

Momentum is different from motivation. Motivation is a spark. Momentum is a river. Motivation can vanish in one night. Momentum can carry you forward even in tough seasons. Momentum is what happens when you do the small work consistently, long enough that discipline becomes normal.

This chapter is about how to build that momentum—how to keep yourself moving, how to reward yourself without becoming lazy, and how to handle missed days without losing hope.

WHY PEOPLE SAY "TOMORROW" (AND WHY IT RUINS MOTIVATION)

Many people don't stop because they hate success. They stop because they fall into a dangerous habit: "I will start tomorrow."

Tomorrow feels safe. Tomorrow feels clean. Tomorrow feels like a fresh start without pain. But tomorrow is also the favorite hiding place of fear.

People say "tomorrow" because:

They're scared of failing again, so they put off getting started.

They fear judgment, so they avoid being seen while learning.

They want perfect conditions, so they wait for a better mood, better time, better resources.

They feel overwhelmed, so they choose delay instead of small action.

People often give up because they don't see things happening right away, and that's when they lose their patience.

But the risk is huge: tomorrow doesn't just delay your work—it damages your identity. Every time you delay, you teach your mind a message: "We don't follow through." And slowly, you stop trusting yourself.

I learned this lesson early. When I restarted my journey, I did not have perfect conditions. I did not have unlimited time. I did not have perfect tools. I did not even have perfect confidence. But I had something stronger than motivation: I had a decision. I decided that my life will not change through wishes. It will change through daily action.

And daily action needs a system—not a mood.

THE REAL PROBLEM: PEOPLE TREAT ONE MISSED DAY LIKE TOTAL FAILURE

This is one of the biggest reasons people lose motivation:

They miss one day, and then their mind says:

"See? You can't do it. You are not serious. You are back to the old you."

They miss one workout and think they failed health.

They miss one study session and think they failed education.

They miss one upload and think they failed content creation.

They miss one writing day and think they failed the book.

This is emotional thinking, not mature thinking.

A missed day is not failure.

A missed week is a warning.

A missed month is a pattern.

It's not about being perfect and never slipping up. What really shows self-control is how quickly you can get back on track after making a mistake.

The strongest people are not those who never fall. They are those who fall and return quickly.

THE MOMENTUM RULE (THE SIMPLE MINDSET THAT KEEPS YOU GOING)

Here is the Momentum Rule:

Never miss twice.

If you miss one day, fine.

You make sure it stays as just one day, not letting it turn into two separate days.

Because two days become a week.

A week becomes a month.

And a month becomes regret.

I've been through a lot, and this rule has been a lifesaver. There have been days when I just didn't feel like I had the strength to keep going. Days when everything felt overwhelming and heavy. Days when all I wanted to do was sleep. But I learned a valuable lesson: if I give up today, I have to start all over again tomorrow. And I mean immediately - not next week, not when I'm feeling better. Right away.

That is how momentum survives.

HOW TO MOTIVATE YOURSELF FOR DAILY TASKS (WITHOUT FORCING YOUR EMOTIONS)

Motivation is not something you "wait for." Motivation is something you create.

Here are the most practical ways to create it:

1) Make tasks smaller, not your dreams

When your task is too big, your brain runs away.

Instead of: "Write a full chapter today,"

Do: "Write 300 words."

Instead of: "Study 4 hours,"

Do: "Study 30 minutes."

Instead of: "Record a perfect video,"

Do: "Record one short message."

Small tasks protect consistency. Consistency protects confidence. Confidence restores motivation.

2) Attach your task to an existing routine

If your task is floating in your day, it will be forgotten.

Attach it to something you already do.

After breakfast → 30 minutes reading

After Asr/Evening → 20 minutes walk

After dinner → 15 minutes planning

Before sleeping → 10 minutes journal

When a task becomes part of a routine, it stops feeling like a burden.

3) Use the "2-minute start"

The hardest part is starting.

So trick your brain: "I will do it only for 2 minutes."

Once you begin, momentum starts. And once momentum starts, continuing becomes easier. This is why starting is more important than intensity.

4) Remember your "why" when your mood disappears

Mood is temporary. Purpose is deeper.

I was feeling really down, but then I remembered why I started this journey in the first place: to pick myself up from a tough spot, to create a new sense of self, and to show myself that it's possible to turn my life around with some hard work and dedication. This reminder gave me the energy to keep going, even when my emotions were running on empty. It's funny how sometimes, when we're feeling low, all it takes is a little reminder of our purpose to get us back on track.

A strong "why" makes tasks lighter.

REWARD YOURSELF (THE RIGHT WAY)

Some people don't reward themselves at all, and then they burn out. Others reward themselves too much, and then they become lazy. Rewarding is not wrong. Rewarding is strategy—if it is done correctly.

A reward should do two things:

1. It should make you feel proud.
2. It should not destroy your routine.

Good rewards:

A favorite meal after completing weekly targets

A movie or outing after finishing a chapter

A small gift after completing 30-day streak

A day trip after completing a major milestone

Bad rewards:

Rewarding yourself before doing the work

Rewarding yourself daily in a way that breaks discipline

Rewarding yourself with something that becomes addiction

The rule is simple: **reward outcomes, not intentions**.

THE CHEAT DAY SYSTEM (SO YOU DON'T LOSE HOPE)

Many people fear cheat days because they think it means laziness. But cheat days can be healthy if they are controlled. A cheat day system prevents burnout and keeps your mind fresh.

Here is a smart cheat day system:

1) Plan your cheat day

Don't let cheat day become an accident. Make it planned.

For example:

One lighter day every 7 days

One rest day every 10 days

One "recovery weekend" every month

A planned break keeps you strong. An unplanned break becomes delay.

2) Cheat on intensity, not identity

Cheat day does not mean you become a different person. It means you reduce pressure.

Example:

If you normally write 800 words, write 200 words.

If you usually spend 2 hours studying, try cutting it down to just 30 minutes.

If you usually work out for 45 minutes, try taking a 10-minute walk instead.

This way, you don't break the chain. You keep the identity: "I am consistent."

3) Never turn cheat day into cheat week

This is where most people collapse. They rest one day and then disappear for seven days. That is why cheat day must have a return rule:

Cheat day ends at night. Tomorrow is normal.

WHAT I LEARNED FROM CONSISTENCY WITH LESS RESOURCES

When I started rebuilding, I did not have everything. I started with limited resources, limited support, and sometimes limited confidence. But I discovered something powerful: when you start with less, you develop the strongest muscle—discipline.

And discipline is more valuable than resources.

Resources can help, but discipline creates resources.

Support can help, but discipline creates progress.

Luck can help, but discipline creates results.

If you can remain consistent in hard days, easy days will become your reward.

THE "RESTART MINDSET" (WHEN YOU MISS A DAY)

If you miss a day, don't do drama. Don't self-hate. Don't write a sad story in your mind. Just restart.

Use this sentence:

I lost a day, but that didn't change who I am.

Then do one small step immediately.

Because the secret is not never falling.

The secret is returning fast.

FINAL LESSON

Motivation comes and goes. But momentum can stay.

Build your momentum with small tasks.

Protect it with "never miss twice."

Reward yourself wisely.

Use cheat days to recover, not to escape.

When your mind tells you to put things off until tomorrow, don't listen - take action today, no matter how small it may seem.

Because the person who keeps moving—even slowly—will always defeat the person who keeps waiting for motivation.

And that is the real comeback:

Not perfect days.

Not lucky days.

Not motivated days.

Just consistent days—until your progress becomes unstoppable.

Work That Fits You

CHOOSE WHAT YOU LOVE—BECAUSE YOUR PROFESSION BECOMES YOUR DAILY LIFE

I have met many people who look "successful" from the outside and feel miserable from the inside. They wear neat clothes, sit in good offices, have a stable salary, and say all the right words. But when you look into their eyes, you see something missing. Their face is tired, their heart is heavy, their smile is forced. They are surviving, not living.

And I have seen this scene again and again—especially with people who spend years in jobs they never loved. Some of them work in banks for decades, not because they enjoy it, but because they were told it is "secure." Their routine becomes a cycle: early mornings, traffic, targets, pressure, meetings, stress, late evenings, and then the same again tomorrow. At first, they try to be positive. Then they become emotionally numb. Then they become frustrated. Then they start blaming everything—boss, system, family, life—

without realizing the real pain is deeper: they are living someone else's idea of success.

A profession is not just a way to earn money. A profession is the way you spend your best hours, your best energy, and most of your adult life. That's why choosing the right profession is not a small choice. It is one of the biggest decisions you will ever make. Because your profession will shape your confidence, your habits, your health, your relationships, your lifestyle—and even the kind of person you become.

Many people choose a profession like they choose a shirt: whatever looks good in society. But a profession is not a shirt. It is a skin. You live inside it every day. If it doesn't fit your nature, it will slowly suffocate you—even if it pays well.

THE BIGGEST MISTAKE: CHOOSING COMFORT OVER CALLING

There is a silent mistake that destroys careers: choosing what is comfortable instead of what is meaningful.

Comfort says, "Pick what is safe."

Calling says, "Pick what makes you strong."

Comfort says, "Don't take risk."

Calling says, "Don't waste your life."

Comfort says, "Just earn."

Calling says, "Earn, but also live."

And here is the painful truth: you can earn money in many places, but you cannot earn back your years.

Some people choose a profession only because of salary, status, and approval. They want people to say, "Wow, great job." They want their relatives to feel proud. They want society to respect them. But what happens when you get that respect and still feel empty? What happens when people clap and you feel no joy? What happens when your career becomes a prison with a nice name?

That is why I say: never choose a profession only to impress people who will not live your life.

WHY PEOPLE END UP IN CAREERS THEY DON'T LOVE

Most people don't intentionally choose misery. They fall into it step by step. And the reasons are usually common:

Some people follow family pressure. They are told, "This is the right career." They never get the chance to ask themselves, "Is this the right career for me?"

Some people follow society's definition of success. They see certain jobs considered "respectable," and they chase that respect even if it kills their peace.

Some people choose because of fear. Fear of uncertainty. Fear of being judged. Fear of not earning enough. Fear of failing. Fear becomes the career advisor.

Some people choose because of comparison. They see friends doing something and they think, "I should do the same." They copy a path without understanding their own strengths.

And some people choose because they don't know themselves. They never develop self-awareness. They never ask: What am I naturally good at? What do I enjoy doing even when I'm tired? What kind of work gives me energy instead of taking it?

If you don't know yourself, you will choose blindly. And if you choose blindly, you will pay painfully.

WHAT I LEARNED FROM MY OWN ROAD

There was a time when my life was not clear. There were phases where I was directionless, influenced by people's opinions, confused about what I should do, and unsure about what I was capable of. When you don't have clarity, life becomes noisy. You listen to ten people and you become ten different versions of yourself.

But slowly, through struggle and growth, I realized something: I was not born to live like a copy. I was meant to live like a voice. I was meant to build impact through ideas, through words, through guidance, through connecting with people. When I began to accept this truth, I stopped trying to fit into every box. I began building the box that fits me.

That is why writing, speaking, research, and content creation became more than hobbies for me. They became the direction of my life. Not because it was easy—because it wasn't—but because it felt right. It felt aligned with my nature.

And that alignment is powerful. When your work matches your nature, you don't need to beg yourself for motivation every day. You still get tired, yes, but deep inside you feel meaning. You feel that your struggle has purpose. You feel that your effort is building something that belongs to you.

THE REAL MEANING OF "CHOOSE WHAT YOU LOVE"

Some people misunderstand this advice. They think "choose what you love" means "choose what feels easy." No. The work you love can be difficult. The work you love can be demanding. The work you love can require sacrifice.

The difference is: when you love it, you are willing to pay the price.

A person who loves his work still gets tired, but he doesn't feel trapped. He may struggle, but he doesn't feel dead inside. He may face pressure, but he feels proud of the journey.

So the real meaning of "choose what you love" is: choose a profession that you can respect, a profession that uses your strengths, a profession that fits your personality, and a profession that you would still choose even if it required patience.

THREE SIGNS YOU'RE IN THE WRONG PROFESSION

You may be in the wrong profession if, deep inside, you feel these things regularly:

You feel stress that has no meaning. Not normal effort-stress, but the kind that makes you feel like you're wasting your life.

You feel jealous of people who are doing what you secretly want to do. Not because you hate them, but because your heart is showing you your real desire.

You feel relief only when the work ends, and sadness when it starts. Your happiest moment becomes Friday evening, and your most painful moment becomes Monday morning. This is a loud signal.

A job can be hard, but if it repeatedly kills your spirit, you must question it.

BUT WHAT ABOUT MONEY AND RESPONSIBILITIES?

This is where reality comes in. Many people have families, expenses, responsibilities. They can't just quit one day and jump into a new world. And I understand that. Life is not a movie.

That is why wisdom is important. The answer is not reckless change. The answer is strategic change.

You don't need to destroy your present to build your future. You need to build your future while managing your present.

This is where most people make another mistake: they keep waiting for a "perfect time" to change careers. But perfect time rarely comes. Responsibilities increase with time. Comfort increases with time. Fear increases with time. And then one day a person says, "Now it's too late."

It is not too late. It is just uncomfortable.

The right approach is: start small, start quietly, start consistently. Build your new direction step by step.

THE "START WHERE YOU ARE" CAREER STRATEGY

If you want to choose what you love, you must first discover what you love—and then develop the ability to earn through it.

This happens through small steps:

First, you explore. You read. You learn. You observe. You try. Many people want clarity without exploration. But clarity comes by doing.

Second, you build skill. Passion without skill becomes frustration. Skill turns passion into profession.

Third, you build proof. A portfolio. A record. A body of work. Not talk—proof.

Fourth, you build income gradually. You don't need to earn everything from day one. You need to start earning something from the direction you love, and slowly grow it.

This is how you move from a job that drains you to a profession that fits you—without destroying your life.

I have lived this truth. When I started building my voice and my work, I didn't start with perfect resources. I started with what I had. I started where I was. I started with small actions that looked insignificant at that time. But small actions repeated become big results. That is not motivation—it is reality.

WHY PEOPLE STAY IN CAREERS THEY HATE

Even after understanding all this, many people still stay stuck. Why?

Because comfort is addictive.

A stable salary can become a golden chain. It gives security, but it can also steal courage. People start accepting stress as normal. They start accepting unhappiness as destiny. They start saying, "At least I have a job." And slowly they stop believing they can build anything else.

Another reason is fear of being a beginner again. In their current job, they feel experienced. In a new direction, they will feel small. They will feel like a student again. And ego doesn't like that.

But life rewards humility. If you are willing to become a beginner again, you can become great again.

A third reason is the wrong circle. Some people are surrounded by those who only understand safety. They discourage risk. They mock ambition. They call dreams "crazy." And if you listen too much, you start shrinking.

That is why your environment matters. When you want to rise, you need voices that understand growth.

THE BEST PROFESSION IS WHERE THREE THINGS MEET

In my experience, the best profession is not only what you love. It is where three things meet:

You enjoy doing it.

You can become excellent at it.

It creates value people need.

If you love something but never improve your skill, you will struggle.

If you're skilled at something but hate it daily, you will suffer.

If you love and are skilled but it creates no value, earning becomes hard.

So choose wisely: love + skill + value.

When this alignment happens, your profession becomes powerful. You feel alive, you grow, and you earn.

A MESSAGE TO THE PERSON WHO FEELS TRAPPED

If you feel trapped in a profession you don't love, don't hate yourself. Many people are trapped—not because they are weak, but because nobody taught them how to choose. Nobody taught them that career is not only about money. Nobody taught them that inner peace matters. Nobody taught them to know themselves before choosing their path.

But now you know.

Start with one honest question:

If money was not the issue, what work would I choose?

Then ask the second question:

What skill do I need to develop to move toward that work?

Then ask the third question:

What is one small step I can take this week?

Small step. Not big drama. Small step.

Because changing your profession is not one leap. It is a series of steps.

THE FINAL LESSON

Your profession is not just a job. It is a daily life.

Choose work that fits your nature. Choose work that you can respect. Choose work that gives you meaning. And if today you are stuck, don't lose hope—build your shift gradually. Learn, practice, improve, and create proof. Start with less resources if you have to. Start quietly if you have to. Start slowly if you have to.

But start.

Because when you choose what you love—and you commit to becoming excellent at it—your life doesn't only become richer.

It becomes lighter.

And a lighter life is the life that rises again.

Happiness First

Most people carry a quiet misunderstanding that slowly steals their best years. They believe happiness is a prize. They believe happiness will come after success—after the job, after the money, after the house, after the degree, after the followers, after the applause. So they postpone happiness like it is something they can collect later.

"I'll be happy when I achieve this."

"I'll relax when I reach that."

"I'll enjoy life after I become successful."

And because of this mindset, they spend their present like a sacrifice and their future like a promise.

The thing is, a lot of people figure this out way too late: being happy while you're working towards something is key, because if you can't find happiness in the process, you're not going to magically feel it when you reach your goal. You can accomplish all sorts of things and still feel unfulfilled, you can climb the ladder and still feel drained, you can come out on top and still feel like something's missing. It's like, you can win, but if you're not feeling alive, what's the point?

Happiness is not just a reward of success. Happiness is a resource for success.

It is fuel.

he biggest lie: "First I will work hard, then I will be happy"

Hard work is necessary. Discipline is necessary. Sacrifice is part of growth. But the mistake is thinking you must live like a robot—dry, stressed, joyless—until you "deserve" happiness.

This is how people become successful on paper and broken in reality.

They build careers but lose peace.

They earn money but lose health.

They gain status but lose relationships.

They achieve goals but lose themselves.

Because when happiness is postponed for too long, success becomes heavy. You may still climb, but you climb with bitterness. You may still win, but you win with exhaustion.

What's really tough to deal with is when you start thinking that stress is just a part of being successful, but the truth is, stress often comes from living a life that isn't true to who you are - it's what happens when you're chasing after success without any real passion or purpose in your heart.

WHAT HAPPINESS REALLY MEANS (AND WHAT IT IS NOT)

When I say happiness, I don't mean fake smiling. I don't mean ignoring problems. I don't mean sitting idle and calling it peace.

Real happiness is inner stability. It is the feeling that your life has meaning, your effort has purpose, and your heart still has hope— even when things are not perfect.

Real happiness is not loud. It is not expensive. It is not dependent on applause. It is a quiet strength that helps you continue.

Happiness is not "everything is easy."

Happiness is "I still have light inside me, even when life is hard."

This type of happiness is really powerful because it gives you lots of energy, makes you more creative, and helps you be brave. It also helps you keep going even when things get tough, and it makes you want to get back out there and try again.

HOW I LEARNED HAPPINESS IS NOT AFTER SUCCESS

There were seasons when my life had no spotlight. No title. No public celebration. No big evidence that my efforts were working. There were days when I was struggling quietly, building silently, trying again and again—while people around me judged me based on what they could see.

If I had waited for everything to be just right before I felt happy, I would still be stuck. The truth is, when you're trying to rebuild after a failure, nothing seems perfect at first. You're working with limited resources, you don't have a lot of support, your confidence is shaken, and there's a lot of pressure on you. But if you wait for everything to fall into place, you'll be waiting forever.

I figured out something really important: I needed a kind of happiness that didn't depend on how things turned out. I needed to be happy with the fact that I was making progress, not that everything was perfect. I needed to feel good about the effort I was putting in, not just about getting praise from others. And I needed to find happiness in doing things that had meaning, not just in making money.

If I hadn't found happiness in tiny achievements, like reading just one more page, or writing one more paragraph, or making a small change to my daily routine, I would have given up. I would have become exhausted and lost my motivation. I would have gone back to my old ways, not because I wasn't capable, but because I wouldn't have had the emotional energy to keep going.

And later, when my work became visible, I understood even more clearly: the happiness I built in silent years was the foundation of the success that came later.

HAPPINESS PROTECTS YOUR CONSISTENCY

People often believe that discipline is the only thing that matters, but that's not entirely true. Discipline is important, don't get me wrong, it's huge - but when you have discipline without happiness, it can start to feel like a burden. It becomes this heavy, painful thing that you're forcing yourself to do, and that's when your mind starts to push back.

Why do people quit so easily?

Because the journey feels like suffering with no meaning.

When happiness is a part of what you're doing, it doesn't feel like a chore. Instead, you feel like you're growing and improving as a person. You take pride in what you've accomplished, and you feel a sense of connection to the reason you're doing it in the first place. It's like a spark has been lit inside of you, and you feel truly alive and engaged.

And when you feel alive, you keep going.

That's why happiness matters: it protects consistency.

A person who is miserable will look for escape.

A person who is content will look for progress.

THE "WHEN I GET IT" TRAP

There is a trap that intelligent people also fall into. It's called the "when I get it" mindset.

"When I get money, I'll be happy."

"When I get fame, I'll be happy."

"When I get the degree, I'll be happy."

"When I get the perfect life, I'll be happy."

But life doesn't work like that.

The thing is, when we finally get what we want, our minds instantly start thinking about the next thing we need to achieve. It's like, we're always looking to the future, waiting for something more. We keep striving for the next level, but somehow, happiness always seems to be one step behind. And that's because we never really take the time to teach ourselves to appreciate the present moment. We're so focused on what's coming next that we forget to enjoy what we have right now.

This is why some people have everything and still feel nothing.

They trained their hands to achieve, but they never trained their heart to live.

WHY UNHAPPY PEOPLE STRUGGLE TO SUCCEED LONG-TERM

Unhappiness is not only an emotion. It becomes a lifestyle. And it creates side effects:

Unhappy people lose energy faster. They feel tired quickly because their mind is heavy.

Unhappy people overthink more. Because anxiety grows when joy is missing.

Unhappy people become impatient. Because the journey feels painful, so they want fast results.

Unhappy people become inconsistent. Because they start associating effort with suffering.

Unhappy people become negative toward others. Because when you're not at peace inside, you see life through a dark lens.

So happiness is not "extra." It is strategic. It is a performance tool. It is emotional strength. It is mental fitness.

THE SHIFT: BE HAPPY TO WORK, NOT WORK TO BE HAPPY

Now let's come to the main idea:

You don't need happiness after work. You need happiness inside work.

Not every moment will be joyful, but your general relationship with effort should be positive. You should feel that work is building you, not breaking you.

Here is the mindset shift that changed my life:

Instead of thinking, "I have to do this," I started thinking, "I get to build this."

Instead of thinking, "This is hard," I started thinking, "This is shaping me."

Instead of thinking, "I'm behind," I started thinking, "I'm progressing."

When you change your inner conversation, your work becomes lighter—even if the tasks remain the same.

HOW TO BUILD HAPPINESS DURING THE JOURNEY

Happiness is not magic. It is a set of habits.

1) Connect your daily tasks to a bigger meaning

A task feels heavy when it feels useless. A task feels light when it feels meaningful. When I worked, studied, wrote, created—what gave me strength was reminding myself: "This is not just work. This is my transformation."

Meaning is the engine of happiness.

2) Measure progress, not perfection

Many people are unhappy because they demand perfection. They keep feeling guilty. They keep feeling late. They keep feeling not enough.

But progress is happiness. When you track small improvement—one more page, one more video, one more step—you feel alive.

Progress creates hope. Hope creates happiness.

3) Celebrate small wins without shame

Some people think celebrating small wins is childish. It's not. It's intelligent. Your mind needs reinforcement. If you only punish yourself, you will stop.

Celebrate finishing a chapter. Celebrate maintaining a routine for a week. Celebrate showing up when you didn't feel like it.

Small celebrations build big consistency.

4) Keep your circle clean

Many people lose happiness because of people around them—constant negativity, constant judgment, constant comparison, constant discouragement.

Protect your mind. Not everyone deserves access to your energy.

5) Keep your body in motion

Happiness is not only mental. Your body affects your mind. When your routine includes movement—walks, stretching, basic exercise—your mood improves, your stress reduces, and your motivation becomes more stable.

6) Rest without guilt

Some people don't rest properly. They either overwork until burnout or rest with guilt until anxiety. Both are unhealthy.

Rest is not weakness. Rest is repair. It keeps your journey sustainable. A tired mind becomes negative. A rested mind becomes creative.

WHAT ABOUT THE DAYS WHEN HAPPINESS IS LOW?

Even strong people have heavy days. The goal is not to "feel happy every day." The goal is to not let one heavy day destroy your whole identity.

This is where a simple rule helps:

Don't put it off if you can't do the whole thing today, just do a little something to get started.

Because doing something protects hope.

And hope is the seed of happiness.

WHY STARTING MATTERS MORE THAN WAITING

Another reason happiness matters is this: happiness grows when you move. When you delay, anxiety grows. When you start, confidence grows.

I learned that waiting doesn't make you feel better. Action makes you feel better. Even a small action.

When you're starting from a tough spot and you don't have a lot, it's easy to think, "I just don't have enough to make it work." But the moment you take that first step, something changes in your mind - you start to realize, "You know what, I'm not completely helpless, I can actually do something about this." And that feeling, it's a powerful one, it brings a sense of happiness because it shows you that you're capable, that you have the power to make things happen.

Power is joyful. Helplessness is painful.

Don't hold out for the ideal time to make a move. The truth is, that perfect moment often doesn't just magically appear - you've got to create it for yourself through taking action and making things happen.

THE REAL SUCCESS IS SUCCESS WITH HAPPINESS

You can be successful and miserable. Many people are.

But the highest success is success with inner peace—success that doesn't destroy your health, your relationships, your values, your heart.

If your success makes you hateful, it is not success.

If your success makes you empty, it is not success.

If your success makes you lose yourself, it is not success.

True success allows you to grow—and still remain human.

FINAL LESSON

Happiness matters for success because happiness is not the prize at the end. It is the fuel on the road.

Happiness helps you stay consistent.

Happiness protects your energy.

Happiness reduces burnout.

Happiness makes hard work sustainable.

Happiness makes progress enjoyable.

Happiness turns effort into a lifestyle, not a punishment.

So don't postpone happiness like it is something you will deserve later. Build it now—inside the work, inside the routine, inside the journey.

Because when you learn to work with joy, you don't just reach your goals.

You become the kind of person who can keep rising again and again.

The Power of a 90-Day Plan

Most people don't fail because they lack talent. They fail because they live with a weak system.

They wake up, react to life, spend energy on random tasks, and then wonder why the year ends with the same results. They have dreams, yes. They have intention, yes. But intention without structure becomes frustration. And frustration is the fastest way to lose hope.

This is why the 90-day plan is powerful: it turns your life from random to focused. It takes your energy and points it in one direction. It takes your dreams and gives them a calendar. It takes your motivation and gives it a system.

A 90-day plan is short enough to feel possible, and long enough to create real transformation. It is the perfect bridge between "I want to change" and "I am changing."

WHY 90 DAYS WORKS BETTER THAN 1 YEAR

People love yearly goals. They sound big. They sound impressive. But for most people, a one-year goal is too far to feel real. When the goal is far, the mind becomes lazy. It says, "We have time." And when the mind believes it has time, it starts delaying.

But 90 days creates healthy pressure. It feels close. It feels urgent. It feels like you must move now. At the same time, it doesn't feel impossible. You can imagine 90 days. You can commit to 90 days. You can fight for 90 days.

The mind handles 90 days better than it handles "forever."

And that is why 90 days creates focus.

THE HIDDEN ENEMY: LIVING WITHOUT A SEASON

One reason people stay stuck is because they don't live in seasons. They live in mixed priorities. They try to fix everything at once—health, money, family, career, studies, social media, personal growth—all at the same time. The result is not growth. The result is exhaustion.

A 90-day plan forces you to choose. It makes you ask: What matters most right now?

When you choose one priority season, your life becomes stronger. Because progress loves focus.

I learned this from my own journey. There were times when I wanted to change everything. But I realized something: if I try to do everything, I will do nothing well. So I started living in seasons—season of learning, season of writing, season of building discipline, season of content creation, season of deeper study.

Each season had one focus. And that focus created results.

WHY PEOPLE SAY "I'LL START LATER" (AND WHAT IT COSTS)

Many people delay a plan because they fear a plan.

A plan exposes you. It shows whether you are serious. It removes excuses. It gives you a mirror. That's why people delay planning. They say, "I'll start tomorrow," or "I'll start next week," or "I'll start when I feel ready."

But delay has a cost.

Delay steals time.

Delay weakens confidence.

Delay increases fear.

Delay strengthens bad habits.

And the worst thing delay does is this: it teaches your mind that you don't follow through.

Once your mind stops trusting you, discipline becomes harder.

In my own life, I had to choose: either keep delaying and remain the same, or start with whatever I had—even with less resources, less support, and less confidence. I chose to start. And starting did not solve everything immediately, but it changed my identity. It made me a person who takes action.

WHAT A 90-DAY PLAN REALLY IS

A 90-day plan is not a long document. It is not complicated. It is a simple commitment to one clear direction.

It has three parts:

1. A clear outcome (what you want by day 90)
2. A weekly structure (how you will move each week)

3. A daily routine (what you will do each day)

This is where most people fail: they only have dreams, not routines.
A dream is emotional.
A routine is practical.
The 90-day plan turns emotion into action.

Step 1: Choose one main outcome

In 90 days, don't try to rebuild your whole life. Choose one main outcome.

Examples:
Finish the first draft of your book
Build a consistent workout routine
Improve English communication
Complete a course or certification
Grow your online platform with a clear schedule
Start a small business or side income

The outcome should be specific. Not "be successful," but "complete 12 chapters," "lose 5 kg," "post 90 videos," "study 90 hours," "save X amount."
When the outcome is specific, the mind becomes clear.

Step 2: Define "the daily win"

Your daily win is the small action that proves you are moving.
If your outcome is to write a book, your daily win might be: "write 800 words."
If your outcome is fitness, your daily win might be: "walk 30 minutes."
If your outcome is study, your daily win might be: "read 10 pages and take notes."

If your outcome is social media, your daily win might be: "record and upload one video."

The daily win should be realistic. Not perfect, but consistent.

Because consistency beats intensity.

Step 3: Create a weekly rhythm

Your week needs structure. Without structure, life becomes reactive.

Here is a simple weekly rhythm:

5 days: deep work days

1 day: light work day

1 day: review and reset

Deep work days are your main effort days.

Light work day is recovery with minimum routine.

Review day is where you check: what worked, what didn't, what to adjust.

This weekly rhythm prevents burnout and keeps you stable.

Step 4: Track progress (the proof system)

A 90-day plan works only when you track.

Tracking is not pressure. It is proof.

Even a simple checklist is enough:

Day 1 ☑

Day 2 ☑

Day 3 ☑

When you see proof, motivation becomes easier. The mind loves evidence. The mind loves streaks. The mind loves progress you can see.

Step 5: Protect your plan from distractions
The biggest enemy of a 90-day plan is distraction.

Distraction is not only social media. Distraction is anything that steals your focus from the main outcome.

People often waste time on things that feel urgent but don't build their future.

A 90-day plan teaches you to ask one powerful question daily:

Does this task move my main goal forward?

If yes, do it.

If no, delay it or drop it.

This is how focused people grow fast.

Step 6: The "missed day rule"
In 90 days, you will not be perfect. Life will interrupt. You may miss a day. The plan must include a rule for that.

Here is the rule:

Never miss twice.

If you miss one day, return the next day. Immediately. No drama. No self-hate. No long guilt.

Because guilt wastes more days than failure.

The plan is not about perfection. The plan is about returning fast.

THE HIDDEN POWER OF 90 DAYS: IDENTITY CHANGE

Here is the most powerful part: after 90 days, you don't just get results. You get a new identity.

You become the person who:

shows up daily

follows a routine

completes tasks

tracks progress
stays focused
returns after setbacks

And that identity is more valuable than the outcome.

Because once you become that person, you can achieve any goal again and again.

In my journey, the biggest change was not one achievement. The biggest change was that I became consistent. That consistency later helped me in study, writing, and building my platform. Results came as a byproduct.

A MESSAGE TO THE READER

If you feel behind in life, don't try to fix your whole life in one week. That is unrealistic and exhausting.

Instead, commit to one strong season: 90 days.

Ninety days is enough to:

build a habit
develop a skill
create a draft
improve health
build confidence
change direction
create momentum

Start with whatever you have. Even if resources are limited, start anyway. The plan is not waiting for perfect conditions. The plan is creating progress inside imperfect conditions.

FINAL LESSON

A 90-day plan is powerful because it gives you clarity, urgency, and structure.

It turns dreams into dates.

It turns motivation into routine.

It turns confusion into focus.

It turns delay into discipline.

It turns effort into identity.

So if you want to rise again, don't wait for a miracle.

Create a season.

Choose your next 90 days—and watch how your life begins to change, one day at a time.

My Night Routine for a Strong Tomorrow

People talk a lot about morning routines. They love the idea of waking up early, drinking water, exercising, planning, and winning the day. Morning routines are powerful, yes—but I learned something even deeper in my own life:

Your morning is only as strong as your night.

The night is where tomorrow is built. The night is where discipline is trained. The night is where the mind is either prepared—or poisoned. And for many years, I didn't understand this. I thought success is only about big decisions, big plans, big actions. But slowly, through struggle, growth, and rebuilding myself step by step, I realized: the difference between a weak tomorrow and a strong tomorrow is often decided in the quiet hours before sleep.

My night routine was not born in comfort. It was born in pressure—when life demanded that I become stronger, when I had limited resources, when I had to rebuild my identity, when I had to prove to myself that failure is not the end, when I was writing and studying and creating content even in the seasons when nobody was watching. Those hidden years trained me. And one of the greatest trainings was this: learning how to close my day properly—so I could open the next day with power.

This chapter is not about a perfect night routine. It is about a real routine that carried me from confusion to clarity, from weakness to discipline, from delay to progress. And if you adopt even a few of these habits, you will feel your life becoming lighter, cleaner, and stronger.

WHY MOST PEOPLE LOSE THEIR NEXT DAY AT NIGHT

Let's be honest: many people destroy their tomorrow at night without realizing it.

They scroll endlessly, and their mind becomes noisy.

They argue, and their heart goes to bed angry.

They overthink, and their brain stays awake even when the body is tired.

They sleep late, and they wake up weak.

They plan nothing, and they wake up confused.

Then they blame the day: "I had no energy. I had no mood. I had no motivation."

But the day wasn't the problem. The night was.

A strong tomorrow is not a miracle. It is preparation.

And preparation begins at night.

THE FIRST PURPOSE OF MY NIGHT ROUTINE: CLOSING THE MIND

When I was rebuilding my life, my mind used to be full. Full of pressure, full of fear, full of questions:

"Will I really rise again?"

"Will people always see me as a failure?"

"Will I ever become successful?"

"Is my effort worth it?"

"Am I wasting time?"

In the beginning, I didn't control these thoughts. These thoughts controlled me. I would go to bed tired but my mind would stay awake. That mental noise is exhausting. It drains your energy even while you sleep.

So I built my night routine for one main reason: to close the day mentally.

A day should end. It should not continue in your head all night.

Step 1: I reduce noise (digital shutdown)

The first habit I built was reducing noise. I learned that a noisy mind cannot build a strong tomorrow.

At night, your brain is sensitive. Whatever you feed it, it absorbs. If you feed it negativity, conflict, random videos, news, drama, endless scrolling—your brain goes into sleep with stress. Then you wake up tired, even after hours of sleep.

So I created a simple rule: the last part of my night must be calm.

This doesn't mean I never use my phone. It means I don't let my phone use me. I don't let the world enter my mind at midnight. I choose what I consume, because what you consume becomes your mood, your thoughts, and your future.

When I follow this, I sleep deeper. When I ignore this, I feel it the next day.

Step 2: I review my day (without self-hate)
At night, I don't judge my day like an enemy. I review it like a student.
I ask myself simple questions:
What did I do well today?
What did I delay today?
What lesson did today teach me?
What is one thing I can improve tomorrow?

This review changed my life because it replaced emotional living with conscious living.

When you review your day, you don't repeat mistakes blindly. You start correcting them. You don't keep failing the same way. You become wiser.

In my journey—from restarting my education to building my voice and work—self-review became my private mentor. Even when nobody guided me, my own honesty guided me.

Step 3: I plan tomorrow (3 clear tasks)
This habit is simple but powerful: I don't sleep until I know what tomorrow needs.

Not a long plan. Not twenty tasks. Only three.

I write down 3 main tasks for tomorrow—tasks that move my life forward.

Some days my tasks are related to study and writing. Some days they are related to content creation. Some days they are related to work responsibilities. But the purpose is the same: wake up with clarity.

Because waking up without clarity is the beginning of wasting time.

When you wake up confused, you spend the first hours deciding, scrolling, reacting. When you wake up clear, you start building immediately.

This habit protected me in difficult seasons. Even on days when life was heavy, I still knew: "These three tasks must be done." That created stability.

Step 4: I prepare my environment

A strong tomorrow is easier when your environment supports you.

At night, I try to prepare small things:

clothes ready

work space clean

book or notes placed

phone on charge

water ready

anything that reduces friction in the morning

This looks small, but small friction creates big delay.

I learned this during my struggle years: if you make tomorrow easy, you will actually do the work. If you make tomorrow messy, you will start your day tired.

Environment is a silent coach. It pushes you or pulls you.

Step 5: I close emotional doors

This is one of the most important parts of my night routine: I try not to go to bed with open emotional wounds.

Sometimes that means I avoid late-night arguments. Sometimes that means I forgive quickly. Sometimes that means I stop replaying what someone said. Sometimes that means I remind myself: "Not everything needs a reaction."

I learned that a disturbed heart produces a disturbed tomorrow.

When you sleep with anger, you wake up with heaviness. When you sleep with peace, you wake up with strength.

So I choose peace—not because life is perfect, but because my future is valuable.

Step 6: I remember the purpose

When a person is rebuilding, it's easy to lose hope at night. Night makes problems look bigger. Night makes loneliness louder. Night makes fear stronger.

So I remind myself: why am I doing this?

Why am I studying?

Why am I writing?

Why am I creating?

Why am I building discipline?

Because I want to rise again. Because I refuse to remain the old version of myself. Because my past failure is not my final identity. Because my life must become proof that a person can rebuild.

This inner reminder is not a speech. It is a quiet sentence. But it keeps the fire alive.

Step 7: I sleep like it's part of success

Many people treat sleep like laziness. But I learned: sleep is not the enemy of success. Bad sleep is the enemy of success.

When I sleep properly, my mind becomes sharp. My mood becomes stable. My discipline becomes easier. My focus becomes stronger.

When I sleep badly, everything becomes harder.

So I respect sleep. Not because I am weak, but because I want to be strong.

A strong tomorrow requires a healthy body. And a healthy body requires rest.

THE BIGGEST LESSON: START TODAY, NOT SOMEDAY

This night routine didn't come in one day. It was built slowly. One habit at a time. One correction at a time. One improvement at a time.

And that is the message I want to give you: you don't need a perfect life to start a strong routine. You need a decision.

Start today with what you have.

Even if you have less resources, start.

Even if your room is small, start.

Even if your life is messy, start.

Even if your past is heavy, start.

Because routines are built in imperfect days.

And when you build a strong night routine, something beautiful happens: your tomorrow stops being random.

Your tomorrow becomes designed.

FINAL WORDS

My night routine gave me something priceless: consistency without stress.

It helped me close the day with peace, plan the next day with clarity, and wake up stronger than yesterday. It helped me become the kind of person who doesn't depend on motivation, but on discipline. And discipline, when repeated, becomes destiny.

If you want a strong tomorrow, don't wait for the morning to change your life.

Change your night.

Because the night is not the end of the day.

The night is the foundation of your next success.

If I Did It, You Can Too

There is a sentence people say that sounds simple, but carries the weight of a whole life:

"Maybe I'm not made for success."

I know that sentence. I've heard it from others, but I've also heard it inside myself—especially in those moments when failure feels like a final decision, when life feels like a locked door, and when the world seems to move forward while you stay stuck in the same place.

This chapter is not written from a stage. It is written from the ground.

From the days when my name meant nothing to the world.

From the days when my results disappointed me.

From the days when people doubted me loudly and I doubted myself quietly.

From the days when I had more pressure than progress.

So when I say "If I did it, you can too," I'm not saying it like a slogan. I'm saying it as a fact built by struggle. Because I did not start from a place of privilege or perfect conditions. I started from confusion. I started from weakness. I started from failure. And I still rose—step by step.

Not because I am special.

Because I refused to stay down.

I WASN'T ALWAYS STRONG

There was a time when I had no clear direction. My teenage years were full of noise. Too many opinions around me, too many distractions, too much influence from people who spoke confidently but understood nothing about my future.

I changed decisions based on what people said. I listened more than I thought. I followed voices instead of vision. I did not have clear goals. I did not have a strong routine. I did not have strong self-belief.

And then came the day that shook me—the day of my high school result.

That day wasn't just about marks. It felt like my whole identity collapsed. In one moment, my mind turned the failure into a lifetime sentence: "This is the end. You'll never rise. You have no future."

People don't understand how dangerous that moment is for a young person. Failure doesn't only test your academics; it tests your hope. And hope is the foundation of everything.

For some days, I felt lost. For weeks, I felt heavy. I remember those moments where you look at the sky and your mind becomes silent—not because you're peaceful, but because you're empty. You start thinking life is finished. You start imagining that everyone was right about you. You start believing that failure is your identity.

But something happened in that darkness: I reached the limit of my own excuses.

I got tired of being tired.

And that is where change begins—not when life becomes easy, but when you become fed up with your own weakness.

I didn't "transform." I started.

People love transformation stories because they look dramatic from the outside. But inside, transformation is not dramatic. It is repetitive.

I didn't wake up one day and become a new person. I just made one decision:

I will give myself another chance.

That was the first victory.

Not a certificate.

Not a degree.

Not fame.

Not money.

Just a chance.

Because most people don't fail because they can't succeed. Most people fail because they stop giving themselves chances.

I started again with small steps. I stopped demanding perfection from myself and started demanding honesty. I looked at my weaknesses and admitted them without self-hate. I looked at my habits and accepted that if I want a new life, I need a new routine.

I didn't have unlimited resources. I didn't have perfect guidance. But I had something stronger than resources: a willingness to work even when I didn't feel confident.

That is the first secret: confidence is not the starting point—action is.

I KNOW WHAT IT FEELS LIKE TO START FROM NOTHING

People see results and assume the beginning was easy. But the beginning was silent.

When I started building my voice online, I didn't start with millions of followers. I started with a number so small it feels almost funny now: 38 followers. I even asked a classmate to follow me so it could become 39. That's how humble the beginning was.

And in those early days, I would record content, edit it, upload it—and then see nothing. Few views. Sometimes almost zero. You work hard and the world doesn't notice. That silence hurts. It makes you question your worth. It makes you think, "Maybe I'm wasting time."

But the truth is: the world doesn't reward your potential. It rewards your consistency.

So I continued.

Not because I was always motivated.

Because I wanted my future more than I wanted comfort.

And the day my first viral moment came, people saw "luck." They saw "overnight success." But they didn't see the 783 times I tried before. They didn't see the hours. They didn't see the discipline. They didn't see the rejection of silence.

The viral moment was not magic.

It was a receipt of consistency.

Later, that consistency became a lifestyle. I kept producing, kept learning, kept improving—until the journey that began with 38 followers grew into 6 million-plus, with approximately 5,000 videos uploaded and still continuing. Not because I never got tired, but because I didn't let tiredness become a full stop.

I know rejection. And I know what it can become.

When I wrote my first book, I didn't receive open arms from the market. I received rejection. Publisher after publisher refused to invest. They didn't see what I saw. They didn't believe the story could become impact.

But rejection does not mean you are wrong. Rejection often means people are judging your future through their limited vision.

One publisher finally agreed to print it—but not to invest in it. I had to take the risk. I had to pay. I had to carry those books home. And even then, people said bookstores won't take it, nobody will buy it, it won't work.

But I believed in something deeper: this book was not paper. It was a decade of my life.

So I offered it to my audience with honesty and emotion. And what happened next proved one thing: when your message is real, it finds its people.

Orders came fast. The books moved. The demand grew. And that once-rejected book became record-selling—reprinted more than 200 times with over 200,000 hard copies printed.

That is why I tell you: rejection is not a wall. It is a test. It asks, "Do you believe in your work enough to continue without approval?"

If you continue, rejection becomes redirection. It pushes you into a smarter route, a stronger mindset, a deeper discipline.

FROM DROPOUT TO DOCTORATE: THE EVIDENCE THAT LABELS CAN BREAK

And then there was the academic journey—the one people love to call "impossible." From being a high school dropout to standing on convocation day holding a doctorate degree, wearing a gown, in the Governor House Karachi—what does that prove?

It proves that your past is not a prophecy.

It proves that the label people give you is not your final identity.

It proves that you can restart, rebuild, and rise—if you keep going.

Even my convocation speech went viral and crossed a million views—not because I was perfect, but because people connect with proof. People don't need motivational words. People need evidence that rising is possible.

WHAT I WANT YOU TO LEARN FROM MY LIFE (WITHOUT PRETENDING LIFE IS EASY)

When I say "If I did it, you can too," I don't mean your journey will be easy. I mean your journey is possible.

But it requires certain decisions:

You must stop waiting for confidence and start moving with discipline.

You must stop needing approval and start building proof.

You must stop fearing failure and start respecting effort.

You must stop looking for a perfect time and start with what you have.

You must stop treating one bad day like a lifetime sentence.

And above all:

You must keep giving yourself chances.

Because a person who keeps trying is dangerous—in the best way. The world cannot defeat someone who refuses to stay down.

A MESSAGE TO THE READER WHO FEELS BEHIND

If you feel behind right now—listen carefully:

Being behind is not shameful. Staying behind is a choice.

You don't need to fix everything today. You just need to start something today.

Start with one step.

One page.

One decision.

One task.

One hour.

One honest attempt.

And then repeat it. Because repetition is how weak people become strong.

Remember: the people you admire are not always the smartest. They are often the most consistent. They are often the ones who didn't quit in the silent seasons.

FINAL WORDS

My life is not a story of perfection. It is a story of restarting.

I fell. I failed. I doubted. I struggled. I faced silence. I faced rejection. I felt small. I had limited resources. I had heavy days.

But I kept moving.

And if a person like me—who began with failure, confusion, and very little—can rise again...

Then you can too.

Not because you are lucky.

Not because life will suddenly become easy.

Because you have something stronger than fear:

The power to begin again.

And that power is enough to change everything.

Your Turn: The Rise Starts Now

I don't know your full story, but I know the feeling.

I know what it feels like when your heart wants a new life, but your past keeps pulling you back. I know what it feels like when you look at others and feel late. I know what it feels like when people's words become heavy stones on your confidence. I know what it feels like when you've tried before and fallen—and now even your own mind starts saying, "Maybe this is just who you are."

But let me tell you something with full honesty:

That voice is not truth.

That voice is fear.

And fear loves one thing more than anything else: delay.

Fear doesn't always shout. Sometimes fear whispers politely:

"Not today."

"Start later."

"You're tired."

"You don't have resources."

"Wait for the right time."

"Fix everything first."

"Tomorrow will be better."

And because the voice is polite, people accept it. They don't realize they are being trapped.

I'm writing this chapter for the person who is standing at the edge of change—feeling hope and fear at the same time. This is not just a chapter. This is a hand reaching toward you, saying: it is your turn now.

Because the rise does not begin when the world becomes easy.

The rise begins when you decide you're done with staying down.

I STARTED WITH LESS—AND THAT'S WHY I BELIEVE IN YOU

There was a time when I had no title to hide behind. No degree to impress people. No fame to make my voice loud. No crowd to make me feel important.

I had pressure.

I had doubts.

I had a past that didn't look "successful."

And I had people who were ready to use my failure as a final judgment.

When I failed in school, it wasn't just an academic moment—it was an emotional earthquake. It felt like the road closed. It felt like the world just stamped a label on me. And at that stage of life, labels can feel like destiny.

For days, I carried shame in silence. For weeks, I carried confusion. I remember moments where life felt like it had stopped, where I didn't even have the energy to dream properly. And when you are in that darkness, the easiest thing in the world is to accept defeat.

But something inside me refused to accept it.

Not because I was already strong—but because I was tired of being weak.

That is where my rise began. Not with applause. Not with confidence. Not with full resources.

It began with a decision: I will not end my story here.

If your resources are limited, I understand you. I started with less too. And that is why I can tell you with certainty: you do not need perfect conditions to start rising. You need courage to take the first step where you are.

The most dangerous habit: delaying your comeback

Many people don't lose because they fail. They lose because they delay rising after failure.

They treat their pain like a permanent home. They sit inside disappointment too long. They wait for motivation. They wait for support. They wait for miracles.

And slowly, "waiting" becomes their identity.

I've seen it in so many lives: someone is talented, but they keep postponing action. They say they will start soon. They say they will change next week. They say they will begin after some problem ends. But problems never end completely. Life always has pressure. If you wait for perfect silence, you will never move.

Here is what I learned: delay does not protect you. Delay weakens you.

Every time you delay, you teach your mind that you can be defeated. You teach your soul that your dreams are optional. You teach your identity that you don't follow through.

But every time you act—even small—you teach your mind a new truth: "I can move." And that truth is powerful. It becomes confidence.

That's why I say the rise starts now—not when everything becomes easy.

MY RISE WAS BUILT BY SMALL DAILY PROOF

People like dramatic stories. They like overnight success. But real life is built by quiet proof.

I didn't rise with one big leap. I rose with small steps repeated until they became my personality.

I studied again when I didn't feel like it.

I learned again when I felt behind.

I kept writing when nobody was watching.

I kept creating content when views were low.

I kept speaking even when my voice felt small.

And slowly, my life began to change.

When I started on social media, I had just 38 followers. That number was so small it could make you laugh. I even asked a classmate to follow me so it could become 39. That was my beginning. No spotlight. No hype. No special advantage.

But I kept posting. I kept improving. I kept showing up. And then one day, a video went viral—and people saw only the result. They didn't see the 783 videos before it. They didn't see the silent effort. They didn't see the emotional struggle of uploading again and again and getting almost no response.

This is the hidden truth: a "viral moment" is often the reward of years of invisible consistency.

Later, that consistency became a platform of millions, with thousands of videos and massive views. But it started from a tiny beginning. It started from one person who refused to quit.

The same happened with my first book. It was rejected by many publishers before it found a path. Even then, the risk was mine. The decision was mine. The belief was mine. And that rejected work later became a record-selling book—reprinted over 200 times, with more than 200,000 hard copies printed.

Why am I telling you this again?

Because I want you to understand: your start does not need to look impressive. It only needs to be real.

THIS IS YOUR TURN—WHAT DOES THAT MEAN?

It means you stop waiting for the "right mood."

It means you stop waiting for someone to validate you.

It means you stop waiting for confidence to arrive like a visitor.

It means you stop waiting for the perfect time.

Because confidence is not a gift. Confidence is proof.

And proof is built by daily action.

Your turn means you do something today that your future self will thank you for.

Not something dramatic. Something consistent.

THE RISE STARTS WITH ONE HONEST CHOICE

Here is the honest choice you must make:

Do you want comfort, or do you want change?

Because both are not possible at the same time.

Change requires discomfort.

Change requires discipline.

Change requires patience.

Change requires doing work when you don't feel like it.

But the reward is priceless: you become a new person.
And once you become a new person, your whole life changes.

A SIMPLE BLUEPRINT FOR YOUR FIRST STEPS

If you feel overwhelmed, don't try to fix your whole life tonight. Start small. Start clear.
Pick one area where you want to rise:
education
health
career
business
content creation
relationships
personal growth

Then choose one daily action:
Read 10 pages.
Write 300 words.
Walk 20 minutes.
Record one short video.
Learn one new skill.
Apply for one opportunity.

Then do it daily for 7 days.
Not to become perfect.
To become consistent.
Because consistency is the real rise.

FINAL MESSAGE

This book is not just a story of my comeback.

It is a mirror.

It is proof that a person can fall and still rise again. It is proof that a label can be broken. It is proof that small beginnings can create massive results. It is proof that you can start with less and still build more.

Now it is your turn.

Not next week. Not next month. Not after the perfect moment.

Now.

Because the rise doesn't begin when the world changes.

The rise begins when you change.

And the moment you decide to take your first step, your life quietly starts rewriting itself.

So take that step.

Your turn has arrived.

And the rise starts now.

A Letter to the Reader Who Wants to Quit

Dear reader,

If you are holding this book with tired hands and a tired heart, I want you to know something first: I understand you more than you think.

There are moments in life when quitting doesn't feel like weakness—it feels like relief. It feels like the only way to stop the pressure. The only way to stop the noise. The only way to stop being disappointed again and again. In those moments, even hope feels expensive. Even trying feels heavy. Even waking up feels like work.

So if you are thinking about quitting—quitting your dream, quitting your study, quitting your effort, quitting your comeback, quitting the version of yourself that is trying to rise—I'm not here to judge you.

I'm here to write to you like someone who has stood on that same edge.

Because I have stood there too.

Not once. Many times.

I have faced days where my mind was screaming, "Enough." Days where silence felt like rejection. Days where the future looked too far and my energy felt too small. Days where people's words cut deeper than they should. Days where my progress felt invisible. Days where I questioned myself, my ability, and even my worth.

So before I say anything else, let me say this:

You are not strange for feeling like quitting. You are human.

But the real question is not whether you feel like quitting. The real question is: what will you do with that feeling?

Because feelings are real—but they are not always right.

QUITTING IS OFTEN A DECISION MADE IN PAIN, NOT IN TRUTH

Most people don't quit because they carefully evaluated life and decided quitting is best. They quit because they are exhausted. They quit because they feel alone. They quit because they are disappointed. They quit because they are afraid. They quit because they are overwhelmed.

And when pain becomes loud, it starts speaking like truth.

Pain says, "This is the end."

Pain says, "You can't do it."

Pain says, "You're not made for this."

Pain says, "Others are better than you."

Pain says, "You're wasting time."

But Pain is not a judge. Pain is a messenger. It is telling you something needs to change—not that your life must end, not that your dream must die.

Sometimes pain means you need rest, not quitting.

Sometimes pain means you need a new strategy, not surrender.

Sometimes pain means you need help, not silence.

Sometimes pain means you need to start again, not stop forever.

I REMEMBER THE DAY I FELT MY LIFE WAS FINISHED

There was a day in my early life that I still remember clearly—the day of failure that made my future look dark. It wasn't only about education. It was the feeling of being labeled, the feeling of being judged, the feeling of seeing disappointment in the eyes of people you love, the feeling of becoming "the example" people use to warn others.

In those moments, you don't just lose marks. You lose confidence. And when confidence is gone, even simple steps feel impossible.

I remember the heaviness of those days. I remember the way time moved slowly. I remember the silence in my own mind. I remember how easy it was to believe that my story was over.

If someone had asked me then, "Do you want to quit?" I would have said yes—not because I hated life, but because I didn't see a path.

But a path appears only after you take the first step.

That is why quitting feels tempting: because quitting requires no steps. It's immediate. It's painless in the short term. It feels like stopping the struggle.

But it also stops the possibility.

And possibility is everything.

QUITTING DOESN'T END PAIN—IT OFTEN POSTPONES IT

Here is a hard truth, but a necessary one: quitting doesn't guarantee peace. Sometimes quitting becomes a different kind of pain.

Because the pain of struggle is heavy, but the pain of regret is heavier. Struggle says, "This is hard right now." Regret says, "I could have become someone."

The pain of struggle is temporary. The pain of regret is long.

I have learned that life doesn't punish you only with failure. Life also punishes you with the memory of what you didn't try.

So before you quit, ask yourself one honest question:

AM I QUITTING BECAUSE THIS IS WRONG FOR ME, OR BECAUSE THIS IS HARD FOR ME?

Because "hard" is not a reason to quit. Hard is often the doorway to growth.

THE WORLD WILL NOT ALWAYS CLAP FOR YOU—AND THAT DOESN'T MEAN YOU SHOULD STOP

One reason people quit is silence. They work hard, but nobody notices. They try, but nobody appreciates. They post, but nobody responds. They study, but nobody praises. They build, but nobody supports.

Silence is painful. It makes you feel invisible.

I know that silence.

When I began building my presence and voice, I didn't begin with crowds. I began with a small number. I began with limited reach. I began with the feeling of talking into an empty room. I recorded, edited, uploaded—and sometimes the response was so small that it felt like rejection.

And the mind plays a cruel trick in that phase. It says, "If people aren't watching, it means you are not valuable."

That is a lie.

Silence does not mean you are worthless. Silence often means you are early.

And being early is not a curse. It is a training ground.

It trains your discipline. It tests your intention. It builds your inner strength. It teaches you to work without applause.

Because the strongest kind of confidence is not the confidence that comes from praise. It is the confidence that comes from private proof.

IF YOU WANT TO QUIT, DON'T QUIT YOUR DREAM— QUIT YOUR CURRENT METHOD

Let me give you a powerful alternative:

If you feel like quitting, don't quit your dream. Quit the version of the plan that is not working.

Sometimes the goal is right but the method is wrong.

Sometimes the dream is true but the routine is unrealistic.

Sometimes the mission is correct but the pace is too fast.

Sometimes you don't need to quit—you need to adjust.

I've had to adjust many times.

When a person is rising, the journey is not a straight line. Sometimes you push hard, sometimes you slow down. Sometimes you try one strategy and it fails, so you try another. Sometimes you remove distractions. Sometimes you rebuild routine. Sometimes you change environment.

But you don't abandon the mission.

You refine the process.

REST IS NOT QUITTING

If you are exhausted, please hear this:

You are allowed to rest.

Rest is not weakness. Rest is repair. You are not a machine. You are a human being. And a human being needs recovery to remain strong.

Some people collapse because they confuse rest with failure. They feel guilty for taking a break. They keep forcing themselves until they hate the journey. And when hatred grows, quitting becomes easy.

So instead of quitting, take a wise pause:

Sleep properly.

Eat properly.

Go for a walk.

Talk to someone who understands you.

Clean your mind from noise.

Return with a lighter heart.

You don't need to run daily at the same speed. You need to keep moving.

DON'T LET ONE BAD DAY REWRITE YOUR WHOLE IDENTITY

Most people don't quit because of one event. They quit because they interpret one event as a life sentence.

One failure becomes: "I'm a failure."

One rejection becomes: "I'm rejected."

One slow season becomes: "I'm stuck forever."

One criticism becomes: "I'm not good enough."

This is emotional thinking. It's understandable—but it's not accurate.

A bad day is not a bad life.

A slow season is not a dead destiny.

A mistake is not your identity.

Your identity is what you choose repeatedly.

When I failed early, people could have turned that into my permanent label. Even I could have turned it into my permanent label. But I learned to separate the event from the identity. I learned to say: "I failed in this moment, but I am not finished."

That sentence saved me.

A REMINDER FROM MY BOOK JOURNEY: REJECTION CAN BECOME PROOF

There was a time when the work I believed in was rejected again and again. People didn't see value. They didn't want to invest. They didn't believe. Rejection can make you bitter. It can make you silent. It can make you quit.

But I learned something: sometimes the world rejects what it doesn't understand yet.

I took a risk when it was uncomfortable. I carried the work when it was heavy. I kept believing when it was lonely. And later, what was rejected became record-selling.

I'm not telling you this to glorify myself. I'm telling you this to remind you: your current rejection is not your final result.

The chapter you are in right now is not the last chapter.

THE "SMALL ACTION" RULE FOR THE DAY YOU WANT TO QUIT

Now, let me talk to you practically.

If today you want to quit, do not try to be a hero. Do not try to do everything. Do one small action only.

One page.

One paragraph.

One message.

One application.

One short walk.

One short video.

One small task.

Small action is powerful on the quitting day, because it breaks the identity of surrender. It proves you still have control.

You don't need a big victory today. You need a small return.

YOUR LIFE WILL NOT CHANGE BY FEELING BETTER—IT WILL CHANGE BY BUILDING BETTER

Many people wait to feel better before they act. But action often creates the better feeling.

When you complete even a small task, your mind gets proof: "I can do something." That proof becomes confidence. That confidence becomes hope. And hope becomes energy.

So if you are waiting to feel motivated, stop waiting. Begin small. Let the beginning create the feeling.

I WANT YOU TO UNDERSTAND WHAT YOUR QUITTING WOULD STEAL

If you quit today, you might feel relief for a moment. But quitting steals many things:

It steals the version of you that could have been stronger.

It steals the pride you would feel after surviving the hard season.

It steals the confidence that comes from finishing.

It steals your future proof.

It steals the story that could inspire others.

Because you don't know who is watching you quietly. You don't know who needs your story. You don't know who will rise because you refused to quit.

Even if nobody is watching, you are watching yourself. Your soul is watching. Your future is watching.

Dear reader, your story is not over

If your life feels heavy right now, I'm not going to give you fake comfort. I will give you real truth:

You may be tired, but you are not finished.

You may feel weak, but you can rebuild strength.

You may feel behind, but you can still rise.

You may feel alone, but your struggle is not meaningless.

Sometimes the reason you feel like quitting is because you are closer to breakthrough than you realize. The mind becomes loud just before a change. The heart becomes tired just before a new level. The old identity fights back when the new identity is being born.

So don't quit on the day your growth is about to show its fruit.

MY PROMISE TO YOU

I can't promise your road will be easy. But I can promise this:

If you keep going—wisely, steadily, patiently—your life will change.

It may not change in one week.

It may not change in one month.

But it will change.

Because no person remains the same when they keep showing up.

And if I—who started from failure, from low confidence, from limited resources, from silent seasons—can build a new life step by step...

Then you can too.

ONE FINAL REQUEST

Before you quit, do this:

Give yourself one more chance.

Not because you are guaranteed success.

Because you are worthy of trying again.

Do one small thing today. Then sleep. Then wake up and do one small thing again. Keep the chain alive. Keep your identity alive.

And one day, you will look back and realize:

The day you wanted to quit was not the end.

It was the turning point.

With respect,
Dr Ali Sherazi

Acknowledgment

All thanks go to God, the one in charge of everything. He's incredibly wise and kind. I'm really thankful to God.

I want to say thank you to my family, especially my parents and my beautiful wife, for being there for me and helping me through tough times. Their love and support mean everything to me. I'm also thankful for my friends, relatives, and teachers who stood by me and taught me important lessons about life. They showed me that when we're patient, humble, and consistent, we can build strong hearts and get through anything. I feel lucky to have them in my life, and I appreciate all the times they were there to guide me and offer a helping hand.

I'm really grateful for all the people who supported me and also for those who criticized me. Their kind words gave me the strength to keep going, and their criticism helped me to learn and grow. I've come to realize that life isn't always easy, and it's okay to stumble sometimes - it's all part of figuring things out and getting back on your feet.

This book was a huge success, first published in Pakistan, a country in South Asia. Thanks to its readers, it was reprinted over 200 times, which is a lot. More than 200,000 hard copies were sold in Pakistan in a short time, making it a bestseller. The book's message also reached people in India, where it was translated, allowing even more people to read it.

Now, this second edition—*Rise Again*—is being published in Australia and will be available worldwide. My hope is that its message travels beyond borders, beyond labels, and beyond all differences of religion, ethnicity, and nationality—because struggle, failure, and hope are human experiences shared by all.

This book is for people who have faced failure, rejection, or felt like they just aren't good enough - but still want to get back up and try again. If what's written here can help just one person find their confidence, get back on track, and start fresh with courage, then it will all be worth it.

I hope God will bless this work and make it something good that helps people become better, stronger, and more positive. It would be great if it could also help them be more responsible and make a good impact on their families, communities, and the world around them.

www.ingramcontent.com/pod-product-compliance
Lightning Source LLC
Chambersburg PA
CBHW030919060726
47591CB00005B/1606